MAKING ORDINARY EXTRAORDINARY

"A must-read . . . this MTV-era story vividly recalls the surreal time when Tamra Lucid's hot mess of a boyfriend became an apprentice to the greatest metaphysical scholar in America, Manly P. Hall. Part witty manifesto, part feminist grimoire, part LA love letter, this book brings to life an unforgettable mystical friendship, and the road to magic it reveals is lined with palm trees, red carpets, and night-blooming jasmine. A very important document for anyone interested in the life and legacy of MPH, especially if they wish for a more intimate portrait of the man and his remarkable relationship with his wife Marie, not to mention the politics and inner workings of the PRS. I've yet to read anything else offering such a wonderfully tender inside perspective."

CAROLINE RYDER, COAUTHOR OF *DIRTY ROCKER BOYS*

"A compellingly written portrait of life with one of the most significant occult voices of the last century—a rare, through-the-looking-glass account of an esoteric circle that quietly impacted the outer world in which we dwell."

MITCH HOROWITZ, PEN AWARD–WINNING
AUTHOR OF *OCCULT AMERICA*

"Lucid provides a keenly observed account of the southern California spiritual milieu, peppered with scam artists, hungry seekers, sycophants, and bright lights. Importantly, Lucid also highlights the often-overlooked and unsung women working in the background, supporting and often funding the male shining stars of the occult scene. This book is a truly unique contribution to the history of esoteric spirituality in California, providing an honest yet touching snapshot of the spiritual milieu of LA in the 1980s."

AMY HALE, AUTHOR OF *ITHELL COLQUHOUN*

"Tamra Lucid's warm, engaging, and illuminating account of her years as Hall's friend brought back memories of a special time and place and reminded me of just how important and eccentric Hall was. Readers coming to Hall for the first time will get an excellent introduction to him from her account. Those, like me, who remember him will enjoy a welcome reunion with one of the twentieth century's secret teachers."

GARY LACHMAN, AUTHOR OF *THE RETURN OF HOLY RUSSIA* AND
THE SECRET TEACHERS OF THE WESTERN WORLD

"A lovely, soul-stirring, and heart-wrenching tale, culminating in the curious severing of the student-teacher relationship and subsequent mysterious death of the master. This memoir brought Manly P. Hall and the everyday workings of his society more fully to life than anything else."

MARY K. GREER, AUTHOR OF *WOMEN OF THE GOLDEN DAWN*

"Tamra Lucid tells a story about the spiritual culture revolving around one particular teacher, Manly P. Hall, but her narrative will resonate with all women who have been rendered invisible in male-dominated metaphysical scenes. This book is the first of its kind in that it humanizes Hall, as opposed to lionizing him or probing his weaknesses. After reading Tamra's memoir, my regard for Hall the man superseded my respect for him as a sage. This is a quintessential LA tale, a wacky tour of the New Age wilds, and a gripping exploration of the pitfalls of personal divinity, as told by a wise-cracking rebel who drifted into the temple off the mean streets of film noir."

THEA WIRSCHING, AUTHOR OF *THE AMERICAN RENAISSANCE TAROT*

"Tamra Lucid's prose is playful, poetic, and magical, befitting a novelist. Her subject matter is the stuff of great characters—captivating and ultimately tragic. Yet, it is all true. Manly P. Hall was an enigmatic genius and the genius of Tamra is the ability to capture that world of Manly and Marie, with all its quirks, its vision, and its downfall. This book is beautifully written and the stuff of legend. Tamra lays it out with grace, humor, and empathy. I highly recommend this book."

NORMANDI ELLIS, AUTHOR OF *IMAGINING THE WORLD INTO EXISTENCE*

"Bitten by the Rosenkreutz bug as much as her subject, Tamra writes amusingly, briskly, and sincerely from experience about her engagement with Hall and his Philosophical Research Society—doubtless a boon to history, but the book's value exceeds its utility. I greatly enjoyed the breadth of the author's sympathies, her humor, vitality, and her modest, sensible approach, all making for a highly attractive, original, and entertaining book about a transitional period in American esoteric history."

TOBIAS CHURTON, AUTHOR OF *ALEISTER CROWLEY IN ENGLAND*

"Writing with a clear-eyed, intelligent, and often hilarious voice, Tamra Lucid tells the story of the fascinating personalities surrounding Manly P. Hall, a legend from a legendary time in LA history. As a character in the story herself, she takes the reader to the heart of it all. Especially recommended: her portrayal of Marie Hall, Manly Hall's wife, and her struggles with the sexism of the time. The world is changing now, and Tamra Lucid is one of its best new voices."

TOD DAVIES, AUTHOR OF *THE HISTORY OF ARCADIA SERIES*

MAKING THE ORDINARY
EXTRAORDINARY

My Seven Years in
Occult Los Angeles
with Manly Palmer Hall

TAMRA LUCID

Inner Traditions
Rochester, Vermont

Inner Traditions
One Park Street
Rochester, Vermont 05767
www.InnerTraditions.com

Text stock is SFI certified

Cataloging-in-Publication Data for this title is available from the Library of Congress

ISBN 978-1-64411-375-2 (print)
ISBN 978-1-64411-376-9 (ebook)

Printed and bound in the United States by Lake Book Manufacturing, Inc. The text stock is SFI certified. The Sustainable Forestry Initiative® program promotes sustainable forest management.

10 9 8 7 6 5 4 3 2 1

Text design and layout by Virginia Scott Bowman
This book was typeset in Garamond Premier Pro with Chillvornia Stamp used as the display typeface

To send correspondence to the author of this book, mail a first-class letter to the author c/o Inner Traditions • Bear & Company, One Park Street, Rochester, VT 05767, and we will forward the communication.

". . . Call me Cassandra for I have preached + prophesied in vain."

FLORENCE NIGHTINGALE

◈

"Even when nothing is happening, nothing stands still. . . . I am not a rock, but a river; people deceive themselves by seeing me as a rock. Or is it I who deceive them and pretend that I am a rock when I am a river?"

NINA BERBEROVA

"I used to like this town. A long time ago. There were trees along Wilshire Boulevard. Beverly Hills was a country town. Westwood was bare hills and lots offering at eleven hundred dollars and no takers. Hollywood was a bunch of frame houses on the interurban line. Los Angeles was just a big dry sunny place with ugly homes and no style, but goodhearted and peaceful. It had the climate they just yap about now. People used to sleep out on porches. Little groups who thought they were intellectual used to call it the Athens of America. It wasn't that, but it wasn't a neon-lighted slum, either."

RAYMOND CHANDLER

❖ ❖ ❖

This book is not a biography of Manly Hall. This is the story of seven years of friendship between a wise old man and the girl whose name he could never quite get right. Some of his history will be told along the way, but I'm no historian. I just wanted to capture the details of a friendship I treasured.

Dedicated to Arthur Johnson for convincing me I should write it. Love to Ronnie Pontiac for the editing and research and for taking me on this ride to begin with. My sincere thanks to Tod Davies, Normandi Ellis, Thea Wirsching, Danny Goldberg, K. Paul Johnson, Jon Graham, Albo Sudekum, Alcvin Ryūzen Ramos, and Amy Hale, for editorial notes and encouragement, and to Waris Hussein for teaching me the art of storytelling. Special thanks to Renee Ravel for the cover photographs, and Edie Shapiro and Kate McCallum for detailed editing.

CONTENTS

FOREWORD

Danny Goldberg

Dr. Martin Luther King once said, "Although we live in the colony of time, our ultimate allegiance is to the empire of eternity." But how to remember this? The concept of a cosmic messenger who conveys energy and wisdom from higher planes of consciousness to mortals shows up in many traditions, most famously as Hermes in Greek mythology and Mercury in the Roman version. Alas, not that many of us have the ability to be in direct contact with such deities, so we have to rely on human messengers—even the purest of whom are human.

It's a risky business, this blending of modern life and mysticism, always only inches away from scandal, egomania, delusion, or despair. But it's also a golden quest made easier by glimpses into the lives of the great ones who also searched for meaning, metaphorical warts and all.

Manly P. Hall, a lead character of Tamra Lucid's memoir *Making the Ordinary Extraordinary,* had some warts on display, but his life and legacy are part of the great chain of the modern American quest for inner meaning. His most influential work, *The Secret Teachings of All Ages: An Encyclopedic Outline of Masonic, Hermetic, Qabbalistic and Rosicrucian Symbolical Philosophy,* was published in 1928, and as Tamra writes, Hall's great "work was distilling the beauty and wisdom he found in rare manuscripts and books into a philosophy of life that was gentle, healthy, and rewarding." He presented a *Cliff Notes* version of obscure works that most of his readers could never otherwise encounter. This memoir, *Making the Ordinary Extraordinary,* is Tamra's own *Cliffs Notes* version of Hall's life and the metaphysical concepts he explored, rendered in the twenty-first-century language of an artist as influenced by punk as by ancient esoterica.

Long before the beatnik poets legitimized Buddhism for rebellious intellectuals in the 1950s, or the Beatles and psychedelics drew millions of baby-boomers like me to examine Hindu mysticism in the sixties, there were small but passionate enclaves of Americans who were captivated by a variety of spiritual ideas outside of the Judeo-Christian traditions. Manly P. Hall was one of several influential thinkers who found fertile soil for esoteric philosophy and practice in southern California in the 1920s, in the wake of the rapid growth of the silent film industry, when there was a growing community of artists looking for new teachers. One of the many things to admire about Hall's work is an awareness of the interconnectedness of diverse spiritual teachings. Tamra's memoir makes his work vivid for the reader unfamiliar with that work.

I first encountered Tamra in the early 1990s, when she was using the handle Sekmet380 as the founder of a riot grrrl message board on AOL, which was, at the time, the most popular internet portal for music fans, especially those into punk rock. I was one of Nirvana's managers and was the target of many anguished (and some angry) comments from fans after Kurt Cobain killed himself. Tamra, who was about to earn credibility as the feminist punk rock singer of the band Lucid Nation, was an incisive and compassionate voice without a hint of inverse snobbery or blame. Her acceptance meant a lot to me.

I had no idea that she and her husband Ronnie Pontiac had worked for Hall during the last decade of his long, extraordinary life. Although on the surface there is a cognitive dissonance to the juxtaposition of feminist punk rock and ancient mysticism, the common threads are an open mind and heart and a rigorous commitment to telling the truth.

When I first heard about Occupy Wall Street I visited to check out the amazing moment myself. Back online, Tamra posted her interview with the first protestor to be pepper sprayed. When following the protest at Standing Rock, many Facebook users could count on Tamra for the latest news and interviews with Water Protectors. I've looked forward to her interviews with me whenever my books were published. Her questions are never superficial. Neither are the documentaries she and Ronnie have produced, one of them with me, a film called *The Gits* about Mia Zapata and her band. Over time Tamra has earned my respect as an authentic artist and activist, and now, with this special and beautifully written book, as an author.

In *The Varieties of Religious Experience,* William James suggests that one quality of a mystical experience is the impossibility of describing it. This phenomenon is one of the major hurdles to any writer who tries to examine metaphysical subjects. Another is the inevitable co-mingling of delusion and self-interest that any spiritual scene attracts. It is one thing to believe that reincarnation exists and quite another to claim knowledge of specific past lives. Even if a teacher has certain kinds of esoteric knowledge or power, they may not be ethically grounded.

It is a challenge to describe a spiritual teacher in a tone that honors their connectivity with the mystic aspects of the universe and human existence and also acknowledges egotism, human foibles, and the tawdry infighting that inevitably surrounds even the best of them. One of my favorite passages in *Making the Ordinary Extraordinary* occurs late in the book when Tamra summarizes her experiences as Hall's designated screener of those who wanted to meet him: "I met many casualties of spirituality gone wrong. The seekers of wisdom who were actually seeking dominion. The ceremonial magicians who opened portals they could not close into realms they could not understand. The positive thinkers whose shadows erupted into inexplicably negative predicaments. The prosperity teachers who never really succeeded at anything. The humble Christians obsessed with self-aggrandizing missions. The white men convinced they were gurus of Eastern lineages. The paranormal researchers who discovered entities that would not leave them alone. The psychics who could not shut down their reception of the thoughts and feelings of others. The hucksters repackaging metaphysical teachings as personality cults. What a world of cliques, competition, and manipulation was revealed!"

Another favorite part of the book is how she deals with the gender inequality that pervaded much of the New Age culture of the twentieth century. Tamra writes of Hall's wife, "If Marie Hall had been born sixty years later and went to Evergreen College in Olympia, Washington, she probably would have started a riot grrrl chapter, a zine, and her own band."

Most writing about spiritual leaders falls into one of two categories: reverent hagiography or disillusioned exposé. But there are a few, such as *Making the Ordinary Extraordinary,* that aspire to synthesize both the "colony" and the "empire" of Dr. King's rhetorical imagining.

DANNY GOLDBERG has worked in the music business since the late 1960s, starting as a journalist for *Rolling Stone, The Village Voice,* and *Billboard Magazine.* He was president of Atlantic Records, chairman and CEO of both the Warner Music Group and the Mercury Records Group, and vice president of Led Zeppelin's Swan Song Records. He formed numerous record labels, including Artemis and Modern Records, and is currently the president of Gold Village Entertainment. Goldberg is also a documentary producer, music consultant, and anticensorship activist. Formerly the manager of Nirvana, in 2019 he published the memoir *Serving the Servant: Remembering Kurt Cobain.* Goldberg is also the author of *How the Left Lost Teen Spirit, Bumping Into Geniuses,* and *In Search of The Lost Chord: 1967 and the Hippie Idea.*

CAST OF CHARACTERS

Mine is a story of fate and chance, of happenstance, and even of romance. A story about how one book changed two lives. This is the story of how I became friends with Manly Palmer Hall.

When eighteen-year-old Manly Hall arrived in Los Angeles in 1919, he strolled on wooden sidewalks. The sheep and the orange trees far outnumbered the human population of the San Fernando Valley. The scent of vast orchards of citrus blossoms graced the golden sunsets. The last dust of the old West settled in the shadows of the canyons.

The grandmother who raised him, whom he always spoke of so lovingly, introduced him to esoterica. He was reading Blavatsky when most kids his age were collecting baseball cards. But when she died, young Manly gave up his job as a clerk on Wall Street to reinvent himself in Los Angeles, where silent movies had built studios overnight. He moved to Santa Monica, California, where his absentee mother had settled after she spent fifteen years as a chiropractor among the gold miners of Alaska.

Santa Monica in 1919 was a perennial carnival by the sea. Just south, people frolicked on Venice Beach under a grove of wooden oil derricks. But in spring, wildflowers bloomed all the way up to the shoreline of Santa Monica Beach. Signs in front of bungalows advertised readers of palms, crystals, tarot cards, bumps on the head,

1

and the stars. Santa Monica Pier was a new roller coaster attached to an old pier, across the street from vacant lots.

Like an orchid in a hothouse, Manly flourished in the humidity of the lucidity of the potential of this little city. His mission, his idea, his dream, was to create a center for the study of the wisdom of the ages, the Philosophical Research Society. It still stands more than eighty years later in a cozy corner of Los Feliz, California, with a library of fifty thousand books and manuscripts that MPH (as he was referred to in affectionate shorthand by his staff and volunteers) collected over his lifetime; the rarest are now in the care of the Getty Museum.

Tall and handsome, with striking blue eyes and a Barrymore profile, early in his career Mr. Hall, as I prefer to refer to him, cultivated a creepy elegance; he could have been cast as Dr. Mesmer the Mad Scientist in a noir film starring one of his many celebrity friends.

Back then, Mr. Hall lived in the Ennis House in Los Feliz, a Frank Lloyd Wright extravaganza described by the architect as Mayan Revival. To me it looks like a Mayan mausoleum and will forever be *The House on Haunted Hill,* starring Vincent Price as Manly P. Hall. But you may know it as the exterior of Deckard's apartment in *Blade Runner.* The foreboding castle overlooks the Los Angeles skyline, conveying authority and elevation. Cracks in the walls, in the shadowy rooms where pseudo-Mayan tiles slowly crumbled, provided the ideal backdrop for Hollywood parties, replete with flashy séances, guest fakirs, and dimly-lit performances of eerie music.

"By a curious circumstance," Mr. Hall wrote in the summer 1990 issue of *PRS Journal,* "I lived in this house for some time rent free because it overwhelmed the new owner." He explains: "In the case of a heavy rain two feet of water accumulated on the roof. The zigzag tiles had never been waterproofed. The water gathered in the zigzags; and in fair weather bees took up residence there."

For a time Mr. Hall was a star. His 1942 lecture *The Secret Destiny of America* set an attendance record at Carnegie Hall. In seventy years as an active writer and public speaker, he authored more than 150 books and pamphlets and delivered around seven thousand lectures. His 1928 masterpiece *An Encyclopedic Outline of Masonic, Hermetic, Qabbalistic and Rosicrucian Symbolical Philosophy* has never been out of print. The various editions have sold over one million copies. It has never stopped being a highly influential book in metaphysical circles.

Mr. Hall's influence shows up in surprising places: from his tome on display in the window of a colorfully painted bookshop in Haight-Ashbury at the birth of Flower Power, to Ronald Reagan's brand of American exceptionalism. But Mr. Hall remains a relatively obscure and misunderstood figure. He isn't as widely known today as are Blavatsky, Crowley, or even his friend Krishnamurti.

I met Mr. Hall in the 1980s, when he was in his eighties. President Reagan told us it was morning in America. But my neighborhood was in mourning. The president refused to speak the name of the disease that devastated the gay community, and the world waited with bated breath to see if the new plague would reach them.

At the time, MTV mesmerized kids all over America with hair metal bands dressed up like carnival crossdressers. NWA and Metallica made them look foolish. Crack cocaine and pagers first hit the streets. The decade of the oversexed and proudly greedy smart-ass ended with the protests in Tiananmen Square and the fall of the Berlin Wall. No search engines. No social media. No smartphones. No tutorial videos. No rare books as convenient as clicking over to Google and typing a few words.

These days, archivists at the Getty Research Institute discuss how to preserve the uniquely occult aura of the Manly Palmer Hall collection of alchemical manuscripts, circa 1500–1825, and the books can be paged through online at the Internet Archive. Art historians use it to research the significance of the esoteric tradition in the evolution of modern art. Meanwhile, the Getty is considering changing the name of the collection to honor the mother and daughter benefactors who funded Mr. Hall's trips overseas to acquire these rare treasures.

At first, Mr. Hall relied on these women as his principal patrons.

Later, book sales and wise investments helped him prosper in his own right. Caroline A. Lloyd and her daughter Alma Estelle were oil heiresses. They held him in such high esteem they gave him a small percentage of their posthumous estates so he could carry on the good work. Their generosity benefited him annually until the last few years of his life.

Returning from a vacation in the United Kingdom, Caroline, her husband Warren, and Estelle befriended a Mrs. Chandler and her son Raymond, who had no money and no prospects. The Lloyds let the Chandlers stay with them at their mansion in Los Feliz. Warren worked as a lawyer for the Los Angeles Creamery. He got Raymond a bookkeeping job there. Raymond made it to vice president before getting fired for drinking on the job one too many times. He became a famous writer instead. Warren liked to end his parties with a session at the Ouija board. In their house, Mr. Hall gave one of his first lectures.

In the PRS library I saw a bronze sculpted by Mr. Hall when he was younger. I imagine Caroline inspired him, since she had studied in Paris with Robert Wlérick, a studio assistant to Rodin. Estelle had an apartment in Paris where she hung out with Man Ray and Hemingway. After Caroline died, Estelle donated two bronze figures by her mother to the Exposition Park Rose Garden in Los Angeles. One of the statues, named Poise, was cut off at the ankles and stolen. The feet remain there to this day, still poised.

As for me, there's not much to tell. My father was a Spivey and a Marine. He served his country by doing celebrity interviews in San Diego where he was stationed. I recently found a newspaper clipping about my dad, the sergeant from Indiana who danced with a Hollywood starlet to Xavier Cugat's band during a war. He later claimed to have built transport crates for nuclear bomb parts in his garage workshop. He was a highly skilled carpenter, but how in the hell did he get a job making boxes for nukes? Even if I'd asked he would have made up some elaborate story. He let no opportunity to tell a tall tale go by.

After I stumbled upon a book by Thomas Sawyer Spivey published in 1904, I realized telling tall tales may be a Spivey trait. The book is called *Lavius Egyptus or The Unveiling of the Pythagorean Senate*. With chapter titles such as "Herodotus Seeks the Rosy-Cross," it's clear Spivey-like liberties were taken with history. So I am not at all sure what to make of Tom's insistence that he knew Mark Twain.

You see, Tom Sawyer Spivey was not named after the famous fictional character. Tom claimed he inspired not only the name but the personality of America's most famous juvenile delinquent. Tom's wife said that her husband would often travel to New York to enjoy the company of his old friend Samuel Clemens. In a book, Tom's grand-nephew wrote that his uncle died a multimillionaire with over one hundred patented inventions. Sure he did.

Being raised by Spiveys, in my case, however, produced a result most disturbing to my family. Not only did I have no aptitude for telling tall tales, when some white lie became necessary in the course of events, I couldn't hide my guilty expression. Even my awkward silence betrayed me. "What the hell is wrong with you?" the angry sibling or parent would demand. "Can't you lie like a normal human being?"

My mother loved waitressing. The daughter of a farmer in Indiana, she spent thirty years in coffee shops, mostly in the middle of Hollywood, directly across from the Cinerama Dome, next to the RCA building. She loved feeding celebrities. The busboys nicknamed her *mamacita*. When her boss tried to retire her, she sued him for age discrimination and won. But she always looked at me like I was born fully armored from my father's forehead. Dealing with me did not check any box on her card. When I was fifteen, she gave up on me being a waitress, even though she thought I could get good tips, if I only changed my attitude; but she knew that was a lost cause. If she had only known about astrology she would have said: "Oh Lord have mercy, my daughter was born with Saturn conjunct the sun," but all she knew was what was looking back at her made her feel uncomfortable.

My life wasn't different from that of most other girls. Absent father. Negligent mother. Alcoholic brother, quick to hit. Bullied and gaslit at school. Always known by my last name. Abducted and nearly murdered. Nothing out of the ordinary.

In my late teens, I worked in the shipping department of a warehouse, as a teller at a bank, a title messenger, a member of a three-person cleaning crew for vacant apartments, and I even apprenticed with an Academy Award–winning makeup artist. Why did I change jobs so much? Abusive customers, sexual harassment; but most of all I could never get over the nagging feeling that I was supposed to be somewhere else. I quit the bank, for example, because I got the opportunity to take LSD in Yosemite. But that's a story for another book.

Rainy April 1, two o'clock in the morning. Parking lot of the legendary and inexplicable Rainbow Bar and Grill on Sunset Boulevard, haunt of rock stars and groupies, but also where Vincent Minnelli proposed to Judy Garland back when it was known as the Villa Nova. In 1972 the new owners named it the Rainbow as a tribute to Judy who had died in 1969.

Everybody seemed very impressed to be there, but I didn't get it. What I did get was that I was on a collision course with yet another very unwelcome experience. Five lowlifes had me cornered. I had nowhere to turn. Who do you think I decided would be my knight in shining armor? Yeah, that guy over there in all black with a glare that could cut glass, standing in the rain, smoking a Black Russian cigarette. I watched as he disdainfully gazed upon the parade of humanity passing before him, like a dashing anime villain. "How noble," I thought.

The look he threw at me as I approached him was more than

a little cynical. I had been warned earlier that night by Mario, the proprietor of said establishment. He saw me looking at Ronnie and intervened. "Listen to me," he said earnestly, "you're a nice girl. Stay away from that guy. He's bad news." I didn't know Mario or why he thought I was a nice girl, especially since I was too young to legally be in his club, but I knew he was wrong. Ronnie wouldn't let anyone hurt me, and he didn't. Within two weeks Ronnie and I were sharing his tiny bachelor apartment a couple blocks up the street from the Whisky a Go Go.

Now in case you wonder if I went to the Rainbow that night thinking about meeting the love of my life, no, I was badgered into going by the acquaintance that happened to cause the bad situation I was trying to avoid. I had recently written in my journal: "There is no such thing as true love."

Ronnie also reluctantly came to the Rainbow that night, with his former drummer, looking for their former guitarist. They were going to get the old band back together. Not a band really, more of an invitation to a second Altamont. Ronnie had given up on love, too, and had more of a sex-for-food-and-liquor operation going, with different girlfriends for different days of the week. That ended abruptly. I brought cats, ferns, spider plants, mismatched plates, and cutlery. I also knew the mysterious art of laundry and how to cook fresh artichokes on a hot plate.

Eventually, I learned that Ronnie had grown up under the scrutiny of a family of Holocaust survivors, living like a refugee in the country he was born in. His parents exercised control to a degree that only children who had survived Nazi authority figures could achieve. Their decision to have an only child late in life worked out for me, but not so well for him or them.

Ronnie's best friends were his parent's silver Standard Schnauzer, books, and the occasional feral cats that dropped in wherever they could find him. Even rattlesnakes in empty lots who shook their rattles at any intruder allowed Ronnie to pass. Coyotes found his presence acceptable. There's a rapport between creatures of the wild in the middle of the city. They know their own. He had read Sartre at twelve years old. Earth First monkey wrencher at thirteen. A budding petty criminal at fourteen. The first goth I ever met. Happiness? For the weak. Ronnie had a plan. To die before age thirty, because, you know, ew, thirty. He was a missionary nihilist with a creepy rock band, daring something terrible to happen.

And yet even in his vortex there were signs. As a boy Ronnie once wandered into a bookshop on the west side where he saw on the display table *Atlantis, Mother of Empires*. That book haunted him. At first he yearned for a copy, but the book was too expensive and much too bulky to shoplift. It took its place in his psyche as the symbol for when he first encountered the occult. Only later did he realize the book had foreshadowed his friendship with Manly Hall. The author was Robert B. Stacy-Judd, the architect of the buildings that house the Philosophical Research Society.

Here's a glimpse of Ronnie just before we met, as written by the boy himself: "As an eighteen-year-old I fronted a band for sold-out audiences in Los Angeles. Our guest list ended with an ominous line: anyone wearing the colors of our biker security gang. The club hired off-duty cops to double their bouncers at our shows, but booked us anyway, because they made so much money on the bar, and our manager was bribing the right people with sex and drugs. I added violence to my repertoire of vices. Mayhem, too. I intentionally crashed my car into another car. I'm grateful I was never able to get a gun, and that no one including myself ever got seriously injured by my antics. Eagerly reading books on mind control, black magic, and, naturally, Hitler, I was intent on creating a movement for the forgotten, our revenge on our peers. At live shows redneck guys with their arms folded took up position on either side of the stage to protect the band. Girls who touched me pulled back their hands in slow motion, making a hissing sound as if burned. When I passed a whisky bottle around, it caused a communion of thrown fists. I was well on my way to being at the wrong end of a very bad scene. Fortunately, I fell in love."

I had found the place I was supposed to be, but as you can see I had my work cut out for me.

MAKING THE ORDINARY
EXTRAORDINARY

For over fifty years on Sunday mornings at 11:00 a.m., a ritual was held in sleepy Los Feliz, California, a faded yet stately suburb of grand old trees and Spanish tile rooftops paled by the sun. For that week's truth seekers Manly Palmer Hall would give an inspiring ninety-minute lecture, without notes, on a wide range of subjects at his Philosophical Research Society, or PRS.

Where Los Feliz Boulevard gently curves down to the LA River, PRS stands on a raised corner above traffic, pitched upward like the bow of a mighty schooner; a sanctuary in plain view, yet hidden. Encountering it is like traveling through the wilderness and stumbling upon an ancient Greek temple, except the architecture is Mayan Revival and the wilderness is Los Angeles.

Mr. Hall's wife, Marie Bauer Hall, would be waiting for him just outside the auditorium stage door. The closest she got to any of his lectures was the parking lot. She waited, passenger door open, ready to roll, in a light blue Metallic 1978 Monte Carlo or another of those late-seventies boxy GM cars. The backseat was like a huge vinyl couch.

A vivacious beauty at eighty, Marie often wore tunics she embroidered herself. She clacked her chunky rings and heavy bracelets on the steering wheel. I believe her platform shoes were partially responsible for her lead-footed driving. Marie drove like a Valkyrie on her way to Valhalla. Red lights and stop signs she seemed to take as annoying suggestions.

She'd swerve out of the parking lot and head down Los Feliz Boulevard in a manner that had even a skeptic like me wondering if Mr. Hall had somehow invoked supernatural guardians around this "old jalopy," as Marie called her car and her body. Perpetually serene, Mr. Hall either knew something I didn't, or he just couldn't see well enough to realize the danger.

Destination Michael's Restaurant, straight down Los Feliz Boulevard, thankfully just a few blocks west. With Marie driving, we were there in no time. What a privilege to be invited. The Halls' Sunday lunch at Michael's was one of the worst-kept secrets at PRS, so a polite never-ending stream of admirers passed by the Halls' table to thank him for that week's wisdom. Most told him the tally of years they had been attending or how far they had travelled. Marie teased him about it in her thick German accent. "Look at him, he loves the attention, the big show off. Don't you, Papa?" Mr. Hall humorously feigned insulted modesty.

Ronnie (or as Mr. Hall knew him, "the boy") and myself (or as Mr. Hall knew me, Tanya) enjoyed numerous Sunday afternoon lunches with the Halls at Michael's. The food was good, straightforward American fare. But what I enjoyed most was the polite conversation, the pleasant banter, and the stories about friends they'd known. Like the time Mr. Hall married Bela Lugosi to his fifth and final wife, whose name was Hope. Or the night Burl Ives sang Christmas songs in their living room. He might share that he just purchased a rare stamp he had been trying to get for years, including the history of the stamp and of its country of origin. He would tell at least one elaborate joke. He loved jokes so much that most of the books he kept by his bed were collections of humor and cartoons.

Marie would ask Ronnie about his latest focus of study. Mr. Hall would provide enlightening commentary or recommended reading. But sooner or later Marie would remind us that none of that nonsense is necessary. She referred to reading books as dust eating. She joked that "Manly, being the reincarnation of the snake in the Garden of Eden, still loves to crawl in the dust."

However, this experience I'm about to share with you didn't happen on a Sunday afternoon. It happened on an ordinary Thursday night. During a week when Ronnie and I had been reading about Apollonius of Tyana, a Neo-Pythagorean philosopher who lived around the same time as Jesus or just after, and rumored to have had equally-impressive mystical powers. The story goes that Apollonius stopped a riot just by standing calmly nearby. Ronnie and I agreed that sounded like pure fiction. So when we accepted an invitation to dinner at Michael's, we intended to ask about this alleged extraordinary historical event.

That night the long line outside was not made up of PRS people. Mr. Hall had to wait like any customer. We were under a brightly lit awning watching for Marie's return after parking the car. A woman held up the line for a moment, politely waiting for Mr. Hall. Her impatient husband grabbed her arm so hard it made her wince.

Seemingly unaware, Mr. Hall stepped between them. The frightened woman took refuge behind him. Every time that man tried to get at his wife, Mr. Hall made a slight move blocking his access to her. That provoked the irate husband who turned his anger from his wife to Mr. Hall, screaming until his face flushed blood red. Ronnie stood sideways, ready to fight. I froze in the familiar panic of my violent childhood.

But Mr. Hall greeted that man's anger with emptiness. He had no reaction at all. He may as well have been gazing at a familiar garden. It only took a moment for anger to turn inward, into self-awareness and shame. The man apologized to his wife, then to Mr. Hall, who never acknowledged him, and then to all of us.

Remorseful, the man took his wife gently by the hand and quietly skulked away. I was afraid for her, but I hoped he had learned his lesson. What a remarkable experience, when sanity prevails if only for a moment. To the best of my knowledge Mr. Hall never practiced a martial art. Perhaps he lived so deeply in the Dao that at that moment outside Michael's Restaurant on a chilly evening in Los Feliz he may as well have been Zhang San Feng, the legendary Daoist master who invented tai chi.

As for Apollonius, Mr. Hall's demonstration of tranquility triumphing over belligerence made us reconsider our skepticism. I'm not saying that Mr. Hall knew what our question was and somehow conjured this event to instruct us. But extraordinary serendipity was a common occurrence around him.

THE BIG BOOK

Let us return to the beginning of the story before we met the Halls or had ever heard of them. Ronnie and I joining our fates, as you can imagine, could have led to all kinds of mayhem. Ronnie was troubled, more troubled than me. We discovered we had the same feeling of having to get somewhere, without knowing where or why. Ronnie was already searching for something better. But his definition needed a little elevation. Maybe the destiny he was feeling might be as something other than a musician who dies young to his everlasting fame, especially since he had never done anything to make himself famous.

Ronnie's parents showed a rare optimism when they gave him money for a haircut on his birthday. Maybe they knew he would spend it on something he wanted, but they didn't wish to appear nice or approving. We promptly went to the Bodhi Tree Bookstore, instead, to find something special in the Used Branch. We were looking for a copy of *Atlantis, Mother of Empires*. No such luck, so we searched for a worthwhile substitute.

Ronnie had taken me to the Bodhi Tree on our second date. I met their mascot, a big ol' ginger cat named Bear. We became friends, a tradition I kept with every Bodhi Tree cat, including Lucia, whose reign ended when the store closed and she was taken home by an employee.

In that converted West Hollywood cottage of a used bookstore, Ronnie found a 1936 edition of a tome with an extremely long title: *An Encyclopedic Outline of Masonic, Hermetic, Qabbalistic and*

Rosicrucian Symbolical Philosophy: Being an Interpretation of the Secret Teachings Concealed within the Rituals, Allegories and Mysteries of all ages. Everybody called it *The Secret Teachings of All Ages,* or simply "the big book." It seemed older than 1936. It looked like something from another century. Ronnie had to put it on lay-away because it cost fifty bucks.

When Ronnie paid it off and brought it home, he went through a life-changing adventure, one chapter a day, and he took me with him. The art and the diagrams alone brought out the artist in me, dormant since childhood. Schools of thought I had never heard of before beckoned like old friends. The secret languages of plants, art, math, science, and music seemed to reveal the meaning behind all.

Each chapter introduced new heroes to my pantheon. I learned what a pantheon was—and I had one! Thrice Great Hermes, Pythagoras, Hypatia, Paracelsus, Jacob Boehme, Francis Bacon, Christian Rosencreutz, and of course, the ever-elusive and yet oh-so-popular St. Germain: people who had lived lives according to the concepts of a more exceptional conscience. People who articulated things I had sensed, but who refused to be bound by the social constructs that cloistered my consciousness.

The subtle harmonies of nature I had experienced had been dismissed by me and by everyone around me as a simpleton's flights of fancy. Now I knew these were the perceptions of a sensitive soul, a gift to be used to better myself and to help others. There was more to life than the physical world. "I like this Manly Hall dude, when did he die?" I asked. Ronnie looked at the author's picture. He resembled a vintage thespian. The date of the book was 1936 and that was the sixth edition. According to the manager at the Bodhi Tree Used Branch, the first five editions were more than twice as tall and had full color plates instead of black and white.

It didn't seem like Manly Palmer Hall would still be among the living. So we were shocked when Loreen, a friend of ours, told us that he was lecturing every Sunday at a place called the Philosophical Research

Society in Los Feliz, just a short drive away. She mentioned a little something about how popular he had been with her girlfriends back in the day, when she was young and touring America as a dancer in carnivals.

When Ronnie expressed doubt that a man like Manly Palmer Hall would engage in such behavior, Loreen laughed. Besides reminding Ronnie that men are men, she explained: "He was single. He was handsome. He'd take weekend excursions with ladies up toward Santa Barbara to some romantic hideaway."

I was preoccupied with the revelation that the woman teaching me etiquette had been a carnival dancer scheming with her friends over how to seduce Manly Hall, so, at first, I didn't notice how quiet Ronnie got. I thought he'd want to drive out there that very Sunday. But no, he didn't mention it again. He just read his book.

MY FIRST SUNDAY
AT THE PHILOSOPHICAL
RESEARCH SOCIETY

When confronted with the idea of facing the author of the big book, Ronnie became apprehensive and rather sheepish. For many Sundays there were excuses. I finally asked him why he was stalling. He explained that his nefarious past would be an open book to everyone he met associated with this man. I reassured him I wouldn't be with him if I thought he was really a criminal.

Driving through the dappled light of the sun peeking through clouds, we were greeted by a chain and a Parking Lot Full sign. So we found a spot down the street. We would walk many times along Los Feliz Boulevard under every kind of sky, but the first time was on a beautiful Sunday morning.

Across the street, Spanish Colonial Revival houses with big lawns looked as if they may have belonged to directors of silent movies. We passed a duplex with a charming courtyard where sparrows bathed in a fountain and moss clung to the bricks under a balcony of red, pink, and white geraniums. The roots of old cedar trees were busy slowly breaking concrete. The weeds flowering purple and yellow in the cracked sidewalk caught my eye. Seniors walking their elderly pets eyed the PRS crowd with open skepticism. At least it made Sunday more interesting for them.

First, we heard the murmur of distant greetings. Then we saw the surprise of the almost pink Mayan-Aztec Revival buildings, with a nod to Ancient Egypt. Later, we would wonder if they were Robert Stacey Judd's idea of the architecture of Atlantis. As we reached the top of the concrete steps we entered into the crowded courtyard. These gatherings of students of the esoteric, enjoying each other's company, had been happening every Sunday for decades. Some were dressed up as if for Sunday Service. Others were more the mad professor types, male and female. Some looked like hermits who would not interrupt their research for anything less than a Manly Hall lecture pertaining to their specific course of study. Some were Buddhists and others Christians, many armchair philosophers, a few Sikhs, even a couple of nuns. Like students arriving for a favorite class, many brought notebooks and pens.

We seemed to be the youngest people there. They were pleased to see us even though they didn't know who we were. We were young people and therefore proof that Manly Hall's wisdom translated across the generations.

Sunlight lit the carved wooden doors of the library. They were obviously based on Buddhist scrolls where colossal Buddhas sit stately above the students who revere them. On the left door a severe Confucius, on the right Plato as Zeus; but I didn't know that yet.

I was distracted by a small yet well-stocked gift shop filled with people. Books, spiritual accessories, and symbolic jewelry in the case up front. A room devoted to the very numerous works of Manly Hall. And a strangely incongruous small shelf of what looked like revolutionary pamphlets, all of them by Marie Bauer Hall.

A plaque outside the auditorium read, "Dedicated to the truth seekers of all time." The portrait of young Manly Hall in the lobby was dashing but had a touch of *The Haunted Mansion* about it. In this nostalgic mirage in modern Los Angeles, I felt a sense of familiarity amid the strangeness of the unknown. It seemed like going to church, but this certainly wasn't my mother's Church of Christ.

With unabashed pleasure in each other's company everyone found their seats. I heard snippets of talk about astrology, auras, tarot, alchemy, and astral bodies. I heard, for the first time, phrases like "the higher self" and "Akashic records" and romantic names like Ramacharaka, Ramakrishna, and Ramana Maharshi. I hadn't yet studied any of it, but these magical words and names were portals to worlds I knew I wanted to explore.

FIRST LECTURE

We found seats and surveyed the scene. Beautiful floral arrangements on stage provided a lovely setting. I noticed a dark-haired guy with a limp glancing at the crowd from the small backstage area; he had the smirk of a musician. He fiddled around with a mic set up next to a big green chair with carved wooden handles. I found out later his name was Arthur Johnson and indeed my suspicions were confirmed, he was a musician. Little did I know then that I was destined for the same despicable fate. Eventually, he would become the person most responsible for convincing me to write this book.

At 11:00 a.m. sharp the crowd settled down. A large white-haired man with a cane moved slowly across the stage to the big chair. He sat down, graciously greeting everyone with friendly nods and waves. Warm round of applause. And then he dove into a ninety-minute lecture, note free, without a pause. Lucid all the way through. Took us all on a little excursion, with proper names, dates, publishers of books, Japanese and Chinese words, little asides about the authors, never a trip-up.

Now for some reason unbeknownst to me, but probably the lingering effects of PTSD, I decided this was not Manly Hall. I thought this was a substitute. Midway through the lecture he looked directly at me and started talking about weeds that grow in the cracks of sidewalks, an apt symbol of the opportunity for the soul to evolve through even the harshest conditions. He articulated what I had just seen walking to the lecture and what I always believed but I didn't dare express, because, when I did, I'd get laughed at. But no one was laughing at him. I thought, "If Manly Hall is half as good as this guy, he must be amazing."

At the end of the lecture, he made a couple of announcements and informed his audience that refreshments awaited them in the court-yard. While the others left their seats, we remained in ours. I turned to Ronnie and asked: "Who was that guy?" He seemed confused by my question.

It turned out Ronnie had the same *he looked right at me and said something directly to me* experience. A classic case of retribution anxiety for ill behavior, Ronnie had caught Edgar Cayce's "Earth Changes" fever from Loreen, the same friend who had told us we could still go see Manly Hall lecture. We were practically on our way to Virginia Beach. Loreen had already moved there. But that old man looked right at Ronnie and mentioned irrational fear of earthquakes as a sign of a guilty conscience. Plucked.

Many people would later tell us about their own uncanny moments when it seemed Mr. Hall was talking directly to them about something that deeply troubled them. Later, when I worked with Mr. Hall, I realized there was no way he could see us in the audience. His vision was very poor by then. We were a colorful collection of blurs out there in our seats, but the right words were going to the right places. Call it guided by a higher consciousness or alignment with the Dao, or call it Zen; whatever you call it, he had it.

THE INNER CIRCLE

Ronnie was very enthusiastic about volunteering at PRS just to be around all that. Hall seemed like a nice fellow to me; I liked the feeling of the place. I thought the old man might be a good influence, quite a contrast from the heinous types Ronnie had been hanging around with. It seemed like a higher-quality adventure.

Not long after, we went back during a weekday to volunteer. First, we met Carol; youthful, friendly, warm, she introduced us to her boss Elda. Elda looked like an ancient Greek philosopher. She had cropped silver white hair and clear blue eyes. I was about to learn that PRS was not a patriarchy. Formidable women ran it and ran it well.

Carol was more the New Age type, though she would one day cause a scandal by wearing brown leather mom jeans to work. Memos resulted. Elda was serious and severe yet never mean, but she also knew when to lighten up. If you won her over, which we soon did, she would reveal her wry wit.

Elda walked us into the library. It was a thrill to be there during a work day. A handful of people scribbled at long tables. We knew the big fella himself was in there behind that door on the right that said "Private." Up the stairs we went to meet Christine, a poised, business-like young woman. Christine was talking to Pat Ervin, the lady who ran the business side of PRS as vice president. She had recently inherited the position from her husband John, a lawyer with a Harvard doctorate who won the UN Peace Medal in 1978.

Pat leaned on her elbow on Christine's desk, smoking her trademark Pall Mall cigarette. A dark-haired Capricorn with posture reinforced by military service, her navy blue and white outfit a call back to the uniform she had worn, she still conducted herself like an officer. She seemed unimpressed, but she let Christine carry on with the interview.

Ronnie volunteered menial labor. Which was fine by me as long as *he* did it. Been there, done that. Christine inquired about more skilled labor. "Do you know how to type?" Me: "Yes." Ronnie: "No." "Do you know filing?" Me: "Yes." Ronnie: "No." "Do you know business machines?" Me: "Yes." Ronnie: "No." It became clear that Christine thought I might have a place at PRS, but Ronnie she pondered. Then she asked: "Do you know any languages besides English?" Me: "No." Ronnie: "Not really." He explained he had grown up around people speaking French, German, Russian, and Polish. Christine seemed more interested. "Can you read those languages?" Ronnie: "With a dictionary, maybe." She took down our phone number.

As we walked to our car, we agreed: Christine must have taken our number out of courtesy. But we were still smiling at having been shown around. We felt we had found a true sanctuary in the city.

APPOINTMENT WITH DESTINY

Next morning Christine called. She offered me a secretarial position at PRS. I asked about Ronnie. Nothing yet. Ronnie's enthusiasm waned dramatically. He no longer felt so eager to volunteer, and certainly I was not going to be a secretary at PRS while he would be left to tend to our apartment and cats. I wasn't that into it anyway. I didn't like working at that bank where I learned the skills PRS wanted.

A few days later Christine called back. Ronnie was giving me the look but Christine wasn't calling about me, she wanted to talk to Ronnie. I handed over the phone. He looked shocked. I was too when he told me he had been invited to meet Mr. Hall the next day. To meet the man who had written the book that so changed our lives was a daunting proposition for a guy who had lived the kind of life he'd led up until then. He was one genuinely nervous novice mystic. What would Mr. Hall think when he looked right through him?

As I drove us to Ronnie's appointment with destiny, I considered that while I was okay with doing some volunteer secretarial work, I had to draw the line.

Elda and Carol showed me around the gift shop, shipping, and clerical troubleshooting. There's the coffee machine. I met Richard de la Barcena, a stoic but witty man. Marvelously low-key. I later found out not only did he take care of shipping and receiving, but he was also Mr. Hall's tenth-degree black belt bodyguard. Before that he'd worked for Sinatra, at least that's what Arthur Johnson told us. You'd never know Richard was a martial artist, a hidden master. There seemed to be quite a few hidden masters, of various kinds, in the PRS crowd.

Meanwhile, Christine took Ronnie through the courtyard door into Mr. Hall's office. There Ronnie faced Pearl Thomas, the white-haired PRS librarian, and her formidable assistant, the perpetually grumpy Alice Buse. There stood Pat, in all her naval glory, and Edith Waldron, who always wore pearls and was a total force unto herself, as well as the great man's secretary. Mr. Hall smiled at Ronnie and said, "Sit down and make yourself miserable," in a voice that was a cross between FDR and W. C. Fields. Mr. Hall slid over a stack of papers.

"So, you understand German and French?" Mr. Hall asked Ronnie. "Not very well," Ronnie responded. Mr. Hall explained that the stack of paper on his desk was called a galley, and it would become the bibliography of his extensive collection of alchemical books and manuscripts. Ronnie confessed that he had neither the experience nor any qualifications whatsoever to take on a task like the editing of an alchemical bibliography. He admitted he didn't know much about alchemy or bibliographies. This apparently amused Mr. Hall, who assured him he'd do fine. Ronnie was quickly whisked out of Mr. Hall's office by Edith.

As Ronnie carried the galley out the door marked "Private" into the library, he found himself confronted by Pat. Pat did not think Ronnie was qualified, so she took the galley from him. Ronnie thanked her and agreed that he could not possibly be the right one for the job. That was that. We were convinced the grand old man must have made a mistake. We went home marveling at this strange new world we had encountered. Ronnie got to meet him! Late that very afternoon the phone rang. Edith this time: "Mr. Hall, Ronnie, 9:00 a.m. tomorrow."

That night we wondered what all this could be about. Ronnie liked to read, but could he actually be a scholar? Even so, how could he accept a job that he knew he couldn't do? We agreed that whatever Mr. Hall said, Ronnie would say no.

The next morning, I proceeded directly to the coffee maker in the mail room while Ronnie returned to Mr. Hall's office. This time only Mr. Hall and Edith were waiting for him. Edith had an amused smile. Once again, Mr. Hall slid the galley toward him. "Young man, from now on you will answer only to me. If anyone tries to take this from you, let me know."

Ronnie told Mr. Hall that he agreed with Pat that he lacked the required skills. Mr. Hall reassured him again, promising to explain each step of the task and personally supervise his work. Mr. Hall convinced Ronnie to take on the bibliography.

I was in the gift shop admiring a precious tea set, getting ready to take advantage of my brand-new employee discount, when Ronnie walked in carrying a pile of paper in a file. "This is the galley," he said, looking a bit shaken. Elda and Carol smiled; apparently they knew all about the great battle of the bibliography. Lines had been drawn. Positions taken up.

We were in a daze at this astonishing turn of fate. As we drove home Ronnie announced that we had to visit some used bookstores for French, German, and Latin dictionaries and books on alchemy. Now he had a mission. To do the best possible job he could, to validate Manly Hall's faith in him. Shelves that once contained everything musical were filled with everything metaphysical.

We had entered an alternate universe, found ourselves at Hogwarts, and woke up to discover a heritage we hadn't known. Not only that, but the maestro who had made all that magic possible trusted Ronnie. I won't lie. It felt good to have my opinion of him validated. The day before, we had been without direction, no future, no culture; now we were accepted into a school of the mysteries where we were given the opportunity to become human beings.

THE JAPANESE ALTAR

Edith took Ronnie under her wing. She was a hip old broad who once ran a bookstore. One of those WWII women who went to work during the war and never stopped, because she liked working. On Edith's cluttered desk was a small paperweight with the slogan she lived up to: "A clean desk is the sign of a sick mind."

Edith had a warehouse full of books, the remains of her store. She met us there one sunny Saturday. She told us to bring boxes. We found row after row of books. She let us look through them, while dust particles glistened in rays shining through the skylights. She led us to books we had missed that she thought we should have. She charged us pennies on the dollar. As we loaded the boxes into the car we marveled at her generosity.

I developed a routine. I'd finish my clerical work early and meander over to the library and into Edith's office. She gave me good advice about everything from astrology to birth control. After a couple of weeks she showed me into the big man's office, where Ronnie introduced me to him for the first time.

The meeting was formal. Edith had her hands on my shoulders like a mom. Edith: "Tamra, like camera." Mr. Hall: "Tanya." Me: "Tamra." But I was to be Tanya more often than Tamra. Ronnie, on the other hand, was dubbed and always remained "the boy."

Edith's door to Mr. Hall's office was always slightly ajar if not wide open, so she could keep an ear and an eye on him. When we weren't talking I'd listen to Ronnie getting instructions from Mr. Hall about the alchemical bibliography. When there would be a lull in the conversation, and we were nearing the time when Marie would arrive to pick up Mr. Hall, Edith would push me into his office with a merry "Look who's here!"

Mr. Hall was handsome, charming, a delightful personality. He reminded me of a giant koi fish placidly floating in the pond that was PRS. Gentle and friendly, he seemed to enjoy my unabashed amazement at the art in his office. A Japanese Buddhist altar, taller than me, of intricately carved dark wood, with tiny shelves, compartments, drawers, and nooks, captured my attention. Exquisite little figures of Buddhist and Hindu deities, small crosses, miniature Tantric *yab yum* statues decorated with precious stones, ivory netsukes, incense burners, ashes from incense, bits of paper tucked into cubby holes, intricate trinkets, and minute treasures inhabited every inch of that altar, the accumulation of many years. That was an active altar; it seemed to have a hum about it, like a scaled-down temple. Way cooler than a hutch full of china.

I realized Mr. Hall's entire office was one big altar, filled with inspiring creations from all over the world. He encouraged me to explore whatever interested me, but I rarely touched any of the objects. I'd point at, and try to describe, some mysterious thing. He'd quickly decipher my gestures and tell me about its meaning and history, and if I listened carefully, the life lesson in the story became obvious.

On one occasion I remember in particular, Mr. Hall talked to Ronnie about meditation. Ronnie and I were having trouble with the fifteen-minutes-twice-a-day routine. Mr. Hall responded by telling us how his daily practice had become *kinhin,* the walking meditation of Zen Buddhism. Any activity, no matter how seemingly mundane, could be approached with mindfulness and open awareness. The only other routine Mr. Hall recommended to Ronnie was the Pythagorean Recollection. Before sleep, review the day from the last activity to the first, looking for what could have been done better.

Mr. Hall always seemed to notice when something grabbed my attention: "What have you found over there?" he'd smile. Once, on a bookshelf filled with mostly *PRS Journals,* I spied a brass cat figurine with a raised paw. Since it was a cat I picked it up (that's what I do with cats) and I brought it to Mr. Hall's desk. He seemed pleased that I had found something wonderful to question him about. He looked it over like a diamond appraiser then took delight in telling me the story of the Beckoning Cat, a legendary feline from Japan who saved the teahouse of his master by beckoning at the front door. I returned the Beckoning Cat back to his proper place on the shelf.

To this day I do not know what possessed Mr. Hall to give Ronnie that job. Or why he allowed me to hang around his office bugging him with questions like a grandkid. "What's this?" "What's that?" "Where did you get it?" "What does this mean?" Not only was I getting a master's class in philosophy, religion, and culture, but I was learning about what was important to him, these objects that he had collected over a lifetime, the things he valued enough to keep with him to look upon every day.

But I did witness one uncomfortable exchange between Ronnie and Mr. Hall. Mr. Hall announced that Ronnie would receive sole credit as editor of the alchemical bibliography. For a kid so young this would be a considerable feather in the proverbial cap. Edith thought Ronnie should be delighted at not only the honor but the opportunity. However, Ronnie protested that he was little more than a proofreader who occasionally added text as directed by Mr. Hall. The real work had been done by Bennett Gilbert. Mr. Hall insisted that Gilbert's work had been simply contract work.

Ronnie suggested that there be no editor. A thank you would be more than enough for him. Mr. Hall told him he was getting the honor whether he liked it or not. He reminded Ronnie that he had never done any work like this and yet he rose to the occasion. He checked every measurement Gilbert made. Ronnie had helped Mr. Hall achieve his vision of the bibliography, something that he had been unable to accomplish with Gilbert. The boy would get the credit and that was that. Ronnie asked that Gilbert be included as co-editor, or at least that he be given a thank you. Mr. Hall declined.

What had Gilbert done to deserve such a fate? He had included information, in the bibliographical notes to the books, about various kinds of bodily fluids used in certain alchemical recipes. Mr. Hall told him to remove them. Gilbert refused, since they were actually of value to scholars. Why censor what was really there? Ronnie's first job was taking out all references to bodily fluids. Ronnie never saw a penny for his work on the bibliography. In retrospect, we're both disturbed at how Mr. Hall compromised him, in a sense, forcing him to become a plagiarist. That prestigious editorial credit would always throw shade on Ronnie's integrity—and on Mr. Hall's.

9 PLUTO

In the parking lot of PRS I kept seeing a car with an unusual personalized license plate: 9 PLUTO. I wondered who the driver was, until one day Ronnie openly scoffed at astrology in conversation with Mr. Hall. He challenged Ronnie to learn enough about it to engage in a debate, then assigned him a teacher named Peggy, who turned out to be 9 Pluto herself. I had tried to cast our charts once and got pretty close. I was glad to meet an astrologer recommended by Manly Hall.

Peggy had a Scorpio smile, like she knew something you didn't, something about you. She gazed at us through her big square glasses. She was the first to read our charts. She didn't try to figure them out by math as I had; she sent off for a chart calculated by a computer service, the latest thing. She assured us Mr. Hall approved of this modern convenience. So there it was, the pie chart that supposedly explained my entire life. I asked her about that license plate. She said it meant she had Pluto in the ninth house, but I didn't know what that meant.

Peggy's first comment when she read our charts was, "Boy, you two must really have some fun!" In case there was any doubt what she meant by fun she added: "I like to look at the dirty parts first." Then this question: "Is there a history of twins in your family?" "No twins in my family," I responded with ignorant confidence. Years later my brother, completing the family genealogy, found that our two ancestors who had come over to America in the seventeenth century were twins, and there had indeed been a history of twins before and after.

Peggy proceeded to accurately tell us about our lives until we were left silent. She told me all sorts of odd details. She knew my parents were old, I was a menopause baby. She knew my mother was an Aquarius. She knew I almost died at age fifteen. She knew I needed security in my life to compensate for my rough beginning. She warned me about my habit of putting people on pedestals, and by god they better not fall off or else. "That's not fair," she said to me earnestly. "Not fair to them or you. You're a Capricorn," she repeated several times, "you'll understand it later. All of it. See this?" She tapped a mysterious symbol in the circle of my chart. "Look at that Saturn."

Assistant PRS librarian Alice, a bespectacled older woman, had a pronounced air of authority. She usually wore the frumpiest of hausfrau outfits. However when dressed up on special occasions in a black pant-suit and flowing white blouse she looked suspiciously like a Puritan. Always serious, sometimes cynical, and usually skeptical, Alice never-theless took a shine to us. Like the other women working at PRS, she was formidable and off-putting until you proved your intelligence. Then she revealed her kindness and down-to-earth wit. Alice took Ronnie aside in the library, pointing out *The Rulership Book* as a good source for students of the language of astrology.

Of course, Edith knew about the astrology challenge and gave Ronnie a small pile of carefully chosen books, including several early editions from C. C. Zain's *Religion of the Stars* set. She wanted to see our charts for herself so we got another lesson in interpretation. She got a kick out of blowing our minds. Knowing Mr. Hall would be inter-ested in seeing our astrological particulars, Edith promptly handed them over. We fidgeted nervously while Mr. Hall sat behind his desk studying them with a poker face. Much to my dismay, he never said a word. Did Ronnie still want to debate? Mr. Hall was kind enough not to ask.

I remember sitting in Peggy's small kitchen in the San Fernando Valley in her classic tract house. Where most people would have had a small kitchen table, she had a well-worn washer and dryer. On the dryer were carefully folded and stacked medical smocks and sheets. In the dish rack, not only dishes dried but also scary looking, specialized eating utensils. A recovery nurse who opened her house to people healing from cosmetic and reconstructive surgery, Peggy brought a new meaning to working at home.

I felt uneasy, but her good-natured warmth comforted me. She was so matter of fact as she returned from checking on a patient. A big gal, she moved with a dervish flair, and her skirt swirled flamenco. As she looked over my chart she made a slow circle with her fingers. Peggy was so capable, so confident, she seemed to be making healing circles with every action she took, but this wasn't choreography, only her natural grace. Soon this would all be gone.

AT HOME WITH
THE HALLS

Edith began encouraging Mr. Hall and the boy to have lunch together, often in the vault, where Ronnie was free to choose any book and ask questions about it. On our drive home Ronnie told me the wondrous stories of the day. Mr. Hall found that after a disillusioning moment in history, like say a world war, alchemical and metaphysical manuscripts and first editions could be bought cheap. People were so cynical they thought all such nonsense worthless.

Mr. Hall, then still in his twenties, received generous support from his patrons and admirers so he could venture across the Atlantic. He returned with treasures that would end up being worth millions of dollars. Books like the alchemical diaries of a sea captain who may have been initiated into a mysterious Rosicrucian school in Africa. Books full of diagrams explaining how the stars and the orders of nature relate, what musical harmony has to do with the process of creation, or how everything in the human body correlates with something in nature. Books that were made in the hope of sharing wisdom despite the risk of censorship, imprisonment, and even death.

The first time I ever heard someone mention Marie Bauer Hall was when Edith referred to her as "Mad Marie." Apparently she embarrassed Mr. Hall so regularly one of his catchphrases had become, "Marie, must you tell all?" It's a phrase that I still use on occasion. In the gift shop

I had noticed the small shelf of books she had authored. She seemed her husband's intellectual equal. In fact, since her books were nearly indecipherable, I thought she might be his better; this seemed a reasonable deduction. Marie was no friend to a comma or a period. "Just look at those run-on sentences and fold-out intricate geometric diagrams," I thought. "She must be thinking some serious shit here."

I met Marie when Mr. Hall invited us over for dinner, an invitation that caused Ronnie to monitor me very carefully. As a former stoner from the Valley, who knows what might inadvertently be spoken among such august company? Please note the projection of his fear that he would be found reprehensible. Conversational prohibitions were listed and gone over repeatedly before and during the drive over.

Los Feliz north of the boulevard had a dreamy atmosphere of many forgotten summers. Palm trees glistened and rustled in the wind. There was hardly any traffic on the small streets where old West, old Spanish, and old Hollywood converged. You could imagine seances in the 1920s under Moroccan lamps in any one of those homes.

The Halls' house was a stately understatement with a Spanish architectural flare. On the left, you could see an ornamental replica of a Japanese tea house in the yard under a double tree made of two rough-skinned pines rising from a split trunk. The blue roof of the ornamental red tea house seemed to reflect the sky. A bonsai tree and other personal touches inspired by Asian gardens gave the entrance a multicultural elegance.

Standing under the covered porch we took a deep breath. On our right we saw an oil painting of a pilgrim approaching a hermit's house having walked the long path from a distant town. Ronnie knocked. Marie Hall swung open the door. She wore platform shoes and a colorfully embroidered black tunic. At five feet and a whisper she was a total firecracker. She looked like a Teutonic Judy Garland. She welcomed us with a German accent that never left the old country, then gave us energetic hugs, her big smile genuinely hospitable.

The living room was beautiful and spotless. Instead of drapes or blinds, shoji screens shaded the sunlight coming through the large windows. There were big gorgeous sofas and chairs with an Asian flair. I expected to see books everywhere but saw only one left on a sofa. A painting of young Marie in a red dress looking *Gone with the Wind* hung on the wall, dominating the living room. Like a witty caption, a small bronze plaque in the corner of the frame read "Caution: High Voltage." She proudly explained that her son from her first marriage had put that plaque there long ago. Two imposing, blue-green, wild-eyed porcelain fu dogs with flamboyant manes and tails guarded the entrance to the small dining room.

On the left, a large porcelain vase decorated with intricate flower designs caught my eye. Marie pulled the lid off and encouraged me to smell the potpourri inside. Mr. Hall had been given the vase and the potpourri as a gift by Tibetan priests who visited once. This particular blend was the original potpourri recipe, preserved for centuries in a Tibetan temple. She gave me a handful to take home. I followed her into the kitchen where she got me a plastic baggie to put the potpourri in. I still have it though it doesn't smell as sweet.

I sheepishly asked her if I could smoke a cigarette, challenging one of Ronnie's prohibitions. Marie had no problem with it. She slid over a beautiful Chinese porcelain bowl and told me it was an ashtray. "That's no ashtray," I protested. "Oh, go ahead," she waved her hand.

Mr. Hall had that office altar, but Marie had a hutch full of the most exquisite Chinese and Japanese china. Each plate and cup a little masterpiece. After we sat down for dinner, seeing my interest, Marie introduced me to a charming cup and saucer set. "Hold the bottom of the cup to the light," Mr. Hall suggested. When I did, I saw the delicate black and white image of a beautiful geisha through the translucent porcelain. I had never seen such a thing before. My gasp was audible.

We had a delightful evening with the Halls; they were so genteel and friendly. He told jokes. She mentioned her work while dismissing his facetiously. Dusty old books, dusty old men, with dusty old ideas.

Except for her own books, of course. And that book I saw on the sofa? Her copy of a work by Sri Aurobindo.

Anything you asked about in that house always led to a story that taught something valuable about history and life. They were people who cared about art and culture, who cared about other people's experiences, who were caring enough to share their own. I had never known people like that. I grew up among the flippant, attending a high school next to a garbage dump. My family's dominant language was sarcasm. At the Halls I felt like I was witnessing civilized life for the first time.

Marie was very physical and animated; nothing frail about Marie. She would hit the table or the chair, punctuating her talk with clicks and knocks of her big rings and bracelets, silver with chunks of turquoise and coral. She'd stand behind Mr. Hall's chair playing with his hair while explaining how she used rubbing alcohol on it, before his lectures, to give it shine and more curl. MPH glanced heavenward like a happy comical cherub. He loved the attention she gave him. Now Marie was clicking and knocking her rings on her husband's head. He looked like a big purring cat.

Ronnie and I had never before encountered such an affectionate relationship among elders. This was the first time I had ever observed a husband bask in the doting of his wife. That kind of love between eighty-year-old seniors, that was a new one for me.

We also enjoyed Mr. Hall's favorite dessert: vanilla ice cream, Cool Whip, and crème de cacao. MPH regarded his bowl, held high on his chest, with an impish expression. He was putting on a performance. Childlike and playful, his theatrics of enjoying the delicious dessert made it that much more a treat.

All evening he joked with me in subtle ways. He cracked me up with a look or a lifted eyebrow. My inappropriate giggling puzzled Ronnie, which only encouraged Mr. Hall to try to get me to laugh again. Marie noticed Ronnie's consternation at what seemed to be my insipid giggling. She turned to Mr. Hall and said: "Stop it, Papa!" His expression of shocked innocence made me laugh again.

As Ronnie began discussing astrology with Marie, who was quite good at it, I noticed that she took a shine to him. She found him intelligent enough that she warned him away from the aforementioned old dead philosophers and dusty books. Mr. Hall pretended to look crestfallen. "Oh, Manly, you know I'm right." Ironically, she gave Ronnie several of her own books to take home. She had decided he could understand her work. He had not yet been contaminated by the old Masons, the Theosophists, or the Rosicrucians and their stuffiness.

As we thanked them for the lovely time, we were told to feel free to drop in and visit. Next time they would take us for dinner at their favorite restaurant. The door closed. We headed for our car feeling like we were walking about a foot off the ground. Driving home we lingered over every detail of the conversations and their house. To think that we had been befriended by two such people was the shock of our lives.

That was the first of many dinners. One of Marie's best dishes, the one I got the recipe for, was zucchini pancakes. Sometimes we just sat and watched TV with them. MTV did not go over well. Mr. Hall commented that the flashing lights, loud music, and drug taking of the music scene mimicked the mysteries, opening the psychic centers of people who didn't know what to do with that kind of sensitivity or how to shut it off. He had seen a lot of that kind of damage in the 1960s.

Marie complained about how people are sex crazed and it makes them stupid. All their brains down in their pants; you know, that kind of talk. Music should be uplifting. Their good friends, John Denver and Burl Ives, were held up as examples of wholesome music makers. I got really quiet. "So Plato was right about censoring music?" Ronnie ventured. Marie dismissed Plato as a renowned hater of women. I myself think of Plato as a bitter old queen, but that's another story.

One evening Mr. Hall told us about his visits with Krishnamurti, who then lived just north of Los Angeles amid the California hillside flora and fauna just south of Santa Barbara in Ojai. They were the young stars of the international metaphysical community. Mr. Hall had great respect for Krishnamurti but they had fun together.

Mr. Hall described how every time he visited the Theosophical compound in his fancy old roadster, Krishnamurti would jump up on the running board where, with a grin, he'd hold on for a fast ride to the house. How the noble matrons of the society must have clucked over the chosen ones.

Mr. Hall and Mr. Krishnamurti were not only both regarded as youthful masters, they were both tall and iconically handsome with dark hair a bit wild, like a couple of mad conductors of metaphysical symphonies. They could have run incredible hustles or given in to ego and created cults. People begged them to take power. But to their credit they never did. They accepted appropriate generosity. They weren't greedy for money or fame. They were both devoted to teaching people to be self-reliant. Did they discuss the secrets of enlightenment? Mr. Hall said they shared jokes, talked about sports and current events, swapped stories, compared notes about their unusual careers. What wonderful conversations these two young men so steeped in wisdom must have had under the whispering oaks of Krotona, and what a pity that none of them were recorded.

Another evening, Mr. Hall told us about his visit to Japan. At the home of his wealthy host, at a meal on a table set with the finest porcelain and silverware, Mr. Hall picked up his fork and knife and did a sleight of hand magic trick for the amusement of the guests. He made his silverware disappear for a moment. Marie chimed in to finish the story explaining that the servers hurriedly took away the fancy silverware, replacing it with cheap forks and knives. Mr. Hall then recounted his eerie arrival to Japan, just after the historic earthquake of 1923, when he was twenty-two years old. He told us he could hear the bodies of the dead bump against the bow as the ship glided into harbor in the gray dawn.

Marie rolled her eyes at Mr. Hall's melodramatics. She told us how she had liberated Manly from strange fascinations. Before she met him, Manly kept the blackout curtains closed in every room. She mentioned his "strange little man servant," without going into details. Marie was having none of it. She walked into his life and opened all the windows. Sunlight filled the rooms and hallways. No more late-night occult obsessiveness. Now there would be a hardy breakfast early in the morning like a decent German household.

Usually at some point in the evening Marie would begin to lecture. As she described her work and the benefit it could be to society, how it could change the mundane into the sublime, she became emotional. "Oh, Manly," she would say, "I get so fired up!" She described all of humanity as one family. As if all of us immature souls could be brought to enlightenment by the power of her revelation.

JAZZ CIGARETTES

That Arthur Johnson guy started hanging around Ronnie. It turned out that Mr. Hall had a jazz ensemble working for him. PRS recording engineer and Mr. Hall's occasional driver, Arthur was a top-level guitarist, backing stars like Lena Horne on world tours. Bookbinder and shipping room supervisor Lynn Blessing was a well-known vibes player who played with Bill Plummer's Cosmic Brotherhood and Gabor Szabo's studio band. In the mid-1960s, Lynn had been a member of Tommy Peltier's Jazz Corps, a house band at the famous west coast jazz club, The Lighthouse. Lynn was a musical mentor to no less a talent than Judee Sill.

How did these jazz-cigarette-smoking hippies wind up at PRS? In 1971, Arthur and Lynn moved into a big Victorian house in Hollywood on Berendo Street just south of Barnsdall Park, then the home of summer musical festivals. Lynn's legendary collection of metaphysical books and manuscripts, carefully gathered from obscure bookshops over many years of touring with artists like Paul Horn, became Arthur's playground. Arthur began collecting, too. They gave the house a name: New Temple of Freedom. To celebrate, Arthur drove to Echo Park where he bought a pound of cannabis for seventy-five dollars. Together they rolled about one hundred joints, leaving them all over the house like Easter eggs. The housewarming party was a big success. Arthur met Judee at that party. They made beautiful music together.

Arthur and Lynn were swinging musicians, high on LSD and deep into Bulwer-Lytton's *Zanoni,* Crowley, and Eliphas Levi, the magus of Paris. They got into ceremonial magick. But then the New Temple of Freedom burned down with not only the rare books but the rare instruments and amps, too. The boys had been messing with salamanders—not the amphibians, the fire elementals. They took it as a warning about hubris and ritual. That's when they gravitated toward PRS. They appreciated Mr. Hall's wholesome message so much they wound up volunteering.

Their compatriot, Dave, not only played bass for *The Tonight Show* band but also for Zappa's Grand Wazoo Orchestra. Dave played bass on many Zappa records. The story goes when he was looking out the Zappa tour bus window he saw a dog pee on the snow. Frank turned Dave's comment, "Don't eat the yellow snow," into one of his signature songs.

The PRS jazz band had gotten together and made a collective decision to check out the new kid. Arthur accepted the mission. He casually started talking to Ronnie. Impressed by Ronnie's sincerity, he began looking out for him like the big brother Ronnie never had.

Arthur quickly understood that despite his bluster, Ronnie was mildly autistic in some situations, and with his own experience of dealing with a severe handicap, Art helped Ronnie face the facts. For instance, when Arthur handed some money to Ronnie and directed him to go buy tickets for all of us to attend a concert of experimental classical music, Ronnie froze. Such a simple task somehow stymied him. Arthur laughed, "Oh, that's how it is." While navigating the steps in his leg brace, Arthur pushed Ronnie up the stairs to the box office. Arthur got another surprise that night as Ronnie melted into helpless giggling at a soprano singing the word *sparrow* in dissonant arpeggios. I slowly sank down cringing in my chair. We left mid performance.

Speaking of helpless giggling, not long after, the old Kalu Rinpoche visited PRS. I say "old" because since then he's died and been reborn. He was a comical fellow. The atmosphere in the auditorium was hushed and relentlessly respectful. But the monk was having a good time. He kept tapping his mic, pranking the pro sound man the organizers had brought with them. People seated around us were quite offended when Ronnie began giggling uncontrollably, off and on throughout the lecture. As they passed each other in the crowd after the lecture, Kalu and Ronnie grinned and exchanged slight bows.

Eventually, Arthur invited us to his monastic cell in Silver Lake. I wonder if he was one of the first hipsters to settle in that hipster mecca. Arthur's room was filled with musical instruments of all ages and a collection of occult and poetry books. Where else could you see an original edition of William Blake's works, the fancy green cloth set with gold embossed decorations, edited by William Butler Yeats himself? Next listen to a live performance of a Barney Kessel solo on a vintage electric guitar, then a Dowland recital on lute. But he was a moody bastard; current girlfriends mattered not. He pined for Patricia Perez, some mysterious woman in France. Whenever he'd visit her, music and poetry would pour out of him like a mockingbird singing in spring. For almost two decades Arthur endured this love separated by the Atlantic Ocean, like a knight on a vigil. Then Patricia married him.

Arthur had been a rough piece of work. As a master musician he often dismissed stars of the moment as "not fit to drink my urine from a paper cup." His favorite refrain about his musical career was "They call you a genius, then they never call you." People he admired, including Mr. Hall, he described as "completely out of their minds." Chain-smoking cigarettes, Art talked out the corner of his mouth, puncturing pomposity wherever he found it, but only occasionally his own.

For example, when one ill-informed Sufi enthusiast showed up, Art, punning on the book title *Mystics of Islam,* gave him the nickname "Fishsticks of Islam." Numerous of the luminous were dismissed as "Dr. Deep." But boy could Art be arrogant. He could dole it out as good as the next guy. Still, he had reason to feel so superior; did Miles Davis ever compliment your guitar playing?

Art's boyhood home in the 1950s had the first color TV in the world, since his dad helped invent color TV. But then Art suffered polio right down to the iron lung. He survived and even flourished except for one leg. His dad never forgave him for being human. Art had to wear that brace on that leg the rest of his life, but, man, he never let that stop him. As a teen he was playing black clubs in San Diego, not just the only white guitarist on the scene, but the only white person in the area.

Arthur told us true tales of the naked nymphs of Laurel Canyon in the 1960s bearing silver trays full of a variety of illegal treats at the house of Stills or some other mainstay of the hippie scene. Skip Battin played bass with The Byrds, the New Riders of the Purple Sage, and the Flying Burrito Brothers. But he also played in a pioneer fusion band in Laurel Canyon, with Arthur on guitar. Their neighbor, Papa John Phillips, came over to complain about the noise, much to the band's amusement.

Arthur had toured with Tim Buckley, Antônio Carlos Jobim, Paul Horn, and Pat Boone; played live with Pavarotti; and recorded with Streisand. He worked for major film and television studios and for cinematic genius Robert Altman. Arthur had played Carnegie Hall, the Kennedy Center for the Performing Arts, the Sporting Club in Monte-Carlo, and the Dorothy Chandler Pavilion, not to mention Shelly's Mann Hole. But his gigs in the last of the Los Angeles joints in Crenshaw were just as thrilling.

One week Arthur would be playing a restaurant on Ventura Boulevard. The next he'd be featured soloist with a symphony. And then there was the time Allan Holdsworth showed up at a cafe where Arthur was strumming standards. He was so entranced with Arthur's musical skills he hired him to play solo to open two Allan Holdsworth Trio concerts, the first one that night. Most people at PRS thought of Arthur as that guy in the Leave Me Alone T-shirt who records Mr. Hall's lectures. They had no clue, and that's how Arthur liked it. It worked in reverse, too. Some people he worked with for years as a musician or writer had no idea that Arthur knew Manly Hall.

As book collectors, Ronnie and Arthur often hunted together. Arthur was a frequent visitor to our apartment. He usually brought a jazz cigarette with him and a book or two to show off. He would read key passages and his latest poems. Ronnie would offer his most recent discoveries. I enjoyed hearing them discuss the inner meaning and nuances of their selected highlights. Encouraged by Ronnie, if not downright pushed, Arthur became a popular lecturer at PRS, speaking on a variety of subjects. He contributed poems to the *PRS Journal,* including "The Wishing Well" and "Plato's High Noon." His holiday performances on lute gave a touch of Renaissance class to Christmas festivities at PRS.

Because of the leg brace, sometimes Arthur moved with difficulty despite his usually unassuming grace. Occasionally he used that awkwardness for dramatic effect. He was a master of blues and jazz lingo, seemingly turning into a gnarled old blues man right before your eyes. Hard to believe that the polite quiet guy at PRS was a mere facade for this salty character from the world of show biz. Or was it the other way around?

THE ALCHEMY OF BAKING

Mr. Hall was awarded an honorary doctorate by John F. Kennedy University. As part of the festivities, a group of students toured PRS and enjoyed the privilege of bunking down on the floor in the Halls' living room. Everyone at PRS kept calling him Mr. Hall. Ronnie switched to Dr. Hall. This would not be the first or last time that Mr. Hall asked us to call him Manly. But when we arrived at PRS we were pretty much Ignorance and Want escaped from under the robe of the Ghost of Christmas Present. We were so grateful and humbled by the opportunities this man had given us I still call him Mr. Hall. Ronnie insisted on calling him Dr. Hall. When Mr. Hall protested, Ronnie told him if anyone deserved an honorary doctorate it was him. And even if everyone else still called him Mr. Hall, Ronnie would always remind him of an honor deserved. Mr. Hall responded by telling us a joke about sharecroppers and a government official from the agricultural department. The official had charts, statistics, and all kinds of facts to show farmers how to maximize productivity. He finished, packed up, and on the way out handed his card to Big Man, the local leader. The sharecroppers were eager to get a look at the official card with the embossed government symbol. One of them asked what the letters meant after the official's name. "B.S.," said Big Man, "means exactly what you think it does. M.S. means more of the same. Ph.D. means piled high and deep." Marie liked that joke. Mr. Hall appreciated the honor and kindness he received, but he was quite aware that he was, as he called himself, a rogue scholar.

One thing that amazed Ronnie about working with Mr. Hall was the way this man in his eighties worked daily on articles for his *PRS Journal,* a pamphlet, correspondence, and a book or two. His multi-dimensional creativity taught us by example that switching from one project to another refreshes the intellectual palate. Mr. Hall would send Ronnie to bring him books from all over the library. Occasionally, Ronnie recruited me for these adventures. What amazed us most was how Mr. Hall not only knew which books contained the quotations he needed, but also exactly where that book would be found in a library of fifty thousand volumes, the color of the cover, and often the page number.

When Ronnie heard Mr. Hall was looking for an artist for some small jobs involving books and a reissue of the *Knapp/Hall Tarot Deck,* he volunteered. For the cover of the paperback reissue of *Adventures in Understanding,* Ronnie drew an elaborate tree with a stylized letter Y on the trunk. When Pat saw the mock-up of the book, she confronted Ronnie. She thought that the symbol on the tree was *T* for Tamra. Ronnie explained he meant it to be the Pythagorean *Y,* a symbol of the crossroads that every life faces. I had the impression that Pat never understood what Mr. Hall saw in Ronnie. However Mr. Hall liked the drawing, so it became the cover of the book. The face of the rather primitive sphinx Ronnie drew for the backs of the tarot deck had a vague resemblance to Marie. Mr. Hall didn't mind that either.

I also wanted to contribute creatively. I soon found that my skill as a baker could be a magical art form. The correct food can tear down walls, bring enemies together, and transmute animosity into affection. The right cookie can open doors, even get a warm smile from Pat Ervin.

It began when Ronnie brought my homemade chocolate chip cookies to lunch in the vault with Mr. Hall. I started bringing small cookie assortments for all, which were met with enthusiasm. Then Mr. Hall asked me to bring samples of my baking to the three o'clock get-together.

Pecan puffs, Florentines, and peanut butter cookies. Carrot bread with golden raisins. *Moosewood Cookbook*'s lemon poppy seed cake, chocolate chip cookies with a little extra vanilla. Oatmeal cookies, no stupid-ass raisins. Nothing out of a can. No pies; I never got the art of the crust. Everyone at PRS welcomed my culinary contributions to their afternoon snacks, none more than Mr. Hall. Edith controlled the cookie plate at all times to avoid the wrath of Marie. The old man could be sneaky and moved with surprising speed and dexterity when cookies were involved. He enjoyed each one with comical relish.

One evening I was leafing through a magazine article about gingerbread houses and a light bulb went on. I mail ordered for special paste food coloring. The bright colors were dazzling. I figured it out for myself, knee deep in royal icing. My kitchen was covered with a quarter inch of powdered sugar. On the ceiling, on the cats, powdered sugar everywhere. A white Christmas in Los Angeles. I had a construction site going on in there. Gingerbread tract homes, but each with a unique twist. I presented the best example of the edible real estate to the Halls at the PRS Christmas party. Then I realized, I needed a job.

NO GOOD DEED
GOES UNPUNISHED

The first five editions of *An Encyclopedic Outline of Masonic, Hermetic, Qabbalistic and Rosicrucian Symbolical Philosophy* were masterpieces of the printer's art, from the sturdy amber slipcases to the oversized pages of color plates and intricate engravings gathered from hundreds of rare books.

After an impish glance at me, Edith mentioned to Mr. Hall that since Ronnie had been in the vault working with the materials that contributed to the big book, perhaps an extra copy of an early edition might be lent to him. We were both overjoyed at the idea of having one of these beauties back home with us to peruse indefinitely. But this was a playful farce as the plan all along had been to give us a copy of the fifth edition. Mr. Hall signed it to Ronnie. Back home we glanced at each other and back at that splendid book, awed not only by its grandeur but by the generosity of the gift.

Soon, however, Ronnie's enthusiasm succumbed to a classic pitfall of metaphysicians: initiate fever. The fever commenced with another gift. Mr. Hall had an extra copy of the beautiful gold-gilt-on-red-cloth first edition of A. E. Waite's *The Brotherhood of the Rosy Cross*. Ronnie solemnly received this gift of Mr. Hall's own copy from his younger years. A critique of the book penciled by the maestro himself was on the inside front cover. It had to be a sign. After all, Ronnie's first two initials? R. C.

What are these initiates? Not your mom's illuminati reptilian over-lords. Are Koot Hoomi and the Invisible Masters of the Theosophical Society, the Invisible College of the Fully Awakened, and the Brothers of the Rosy Cross more than just great band names? Frau Anna Sprengel: is the hoax her or the Golden Dawn or both? But can anyone be absolutely certain that there are no ascended masters who live on breath and light or have no need of sustenance because they are beyond the illusion of mortality, reflecting the merest image of themselves into our world? Doesn't seem likely, but you can't prove they don't exist, can you? I can't. It sure makes a good story.

It didn't help that the jazz musicians were checking Ronnie's gull-ibility level, as musicians will. Lynn Blessing told Ronnie that cleaning Mr. Hall's wastebasket he found crumpled up notes in ballpoint pen signed by Paracelsus. Ronnie and I laughed at the preposterous idea of office memos from ascended masters, but I knew he was hooked.

As always, the fate of the future depended upon the virtue of the candidate. Which involved ridiculous prohibitions. Thanks to my will-ingness to take the blame, celibacy could be misplaced easily in our home. But owning a television was a much more difficult challenge. That damn rock and roll music was completely out the door, even though Edith told us how Elvis Presley wanted a signed copy of *The Secret Teachings of All Ages*. Priscilla, and the king's hairdresser Larry Geller, were sent to PRS to accomplish the mission.

Now this is how initiate fever impacts the lives of ordinary people: One fateful night, Ronnie went by himself to the Bodhi Tree to get a book. He returned with a woman, her daughter, and an incred-ible story of reincarnation. Standing before me was none other than Queen Elizabeth I. Her majesty had nowhere to stay. But Ronnie had to prove that whatever the universe threw at him he would meet with open hand and open door. That's what the initiates would want him to do. Neither of us had ever seen an initiate, but of course, they are invisible.

Here was a disturbing turn. As Peggy had pointed out in my

astrological chart, personal safety is a big issue, since I grew up deprived of such comfort. Now I had strangers sleeping just a few feet away. For several days I tried to be patient. But as she took over my kitchen and bathroom, she told stories of stolen secrets, free energy fusion fortunes, and shadow governments. She tried to recruit us to do her bidding. I realized she had to go. But Ronnie refused. He would lose any status he may have gained with the initiates. So I played my only card. I wanted to ask the Halls what they thought of the situation.

To demonstrate his rationality and my hysteria Ronnie proceeded to discuss with the queen her change of venue. To his alarm, he realized she was an expert at this kind of hustle. So we left these strangers in our home with our cats and around eight in the evening drove through a rainstorm to the Halls. We hurried up to the front door like a couple of wet felines.

They took us into a seldom used small side room. Mr. Hall sat with his back to the window, with Marie beside him. The room was dark. As Ronnie's explanation reached the Queen Elizabeth part, the Halls couldn't suppress giggles. Marie became agitated about how we were being taken advantage of. More laughter followed as Ronnie continued, until Mr. Hall stopped him by raising his hand. "This is what you do," Mr. Hall said. "You go right back home and tell her to leave. Tell her I told you to tell her to leave, and if she refuses then you call the police." Lightning lit up the room like an old Hollywood melodrama. That was the first but not the last time I heard Mr. Hall wryly comment, "No good deed goes unpunished."

When we came home her paperwork was strewn across our apartment as if she had built a fort. She seemed surprised when we reported Mr. Hall's verdict. Resentful and resolute, she called her next victim, then began packing. Ronnie tried to warn the man who picked her up in a luxury car within the hour, but he thought we were monsters for kicking a mother and child out into the rain. That poor kid. I asked her if I should call the authorities. She said she had to take care of her mother, or her mother would end up institutionalized. I told her to be sure to get free of her someday. The way I got free from mine. I couldn't figure out a way to help her.

Sometime later, in a conversation Ronnie had with Mr. Hall, the subject of initiates and initiation came up. Mr. Hall told Ronnie he somewhat regretted the emphasis he had placed on initiates in his early days. While I can't prove it, I believe that a telling paragraph in one of the last books Mr. Hall worked on may have been the result of that conversation; it certainly reflects its content. In *The Rosicrucians and Master Christoph Schlegel: Hermetic Roots of America,* Mr. Hall wrote: "We may have sought in the wrong places for the brothers of the Rosy Cross. The temple of this Mystical Fraternity is in our own hearts and, when we make a conscious dedication to the reformation of our lives, we become citizens in the empire of the self-redeemed. It is only in this way that lasting peace can come to this troubled world."

Ronnie set aside his obsession with initiation. But not before he convinced me to try to live up to the Great Renunciation for one week. This was a pathetic exercise in futility. We didn't last the day. But over time we would explore each renunciation on its own: vows of silence, dietary restrictions, days of mindfulness, nights of seeking wisdom from dreams.

FABULOUS CREATURES

Edith gave me an early edition of *Undine* one afternoon. The tipped-in plates of beautiful illustrations by Arthur Rackham adorned a poignant fable about how love is lost: a cautionary tale of what constitutes abuse. So began my collection of books on fairy lore.

Edith told me that all the principles of astrology and alchemy could be found in fairy tales. Mr. Hall pointed out that there were times when wisdom and truth were frowned upon by those in power, so people took extraordinary measures to share knowledge. Consider Ethan Allen Hitchcock, one of Abraham Lincoln's generals, author of an anonymous book on alchemy and another called *The Red Book of Appin,* where he attempted to explain the secret language of folklore. According to Hitchcock, the orphan boy in one story is actually Melchizedek, King of Salem and Priest of the Most High. A dragon in another is the beast of Revelations. Both sets of metaphors, fairy tale and biblical, tell the story of the awakening of the soul. Mr. Hall added that PRS had just published a reprint of the *Red Book of Appin,* available at a very reasonable price in the gift shop.

Collecting fairy books became my metaphysical specialty. But as I read the books and studied the illustrations, fairy tale characters seemed to appear in my life—fey creatures perhaps not entirely human. For example, as I helped out in the office one day, a memo came down from Pat Ervin. Her new assistant was named Marianne Williamson and we should all take note of the correct spelling. A studious girl on a mission, Marianne started lecturing about *A Course in Miracles* and her career skyrocketed. She found her own flock. What Marianne went on to do with Project Angel Food in the early days of AIDS hitting LA was holy. We never really talked until years later when she first ran for office. I interviewed her for *Newtopia Magazine*. I still marvel at her call to service. But she does look like an elf.

Sometimes Richard de la Barcena and I took a smoking break. He would tell me stories about PRS twenty years before, when volunteers were plentiful and the business prospered. He encouraged me to use common sense when dealing with the metaphysical. People with all sorts of strange ideas had passed through PRS. He believed what they were really looking for was glamour. "The glamour of magic, the glamour of the spirits." That had nothing to do with Mr. Hall. Richard summarized Mr. Hall's message as: "Live a better life, truly enjoy life, by cultivating tranquility. That's when everything becomes clear."

Then there was Mr. Louis who visited us several times. A polite and gentle man, he always spoke in a hushed voice. He would find an out-of-the-way corner in our apartment, sit down, and meditate. That is definitely a strange behavior, but his self-contained calm made the visits pleasant. Ronnie and I tried to get him refreshments. He refused them. We tried to engage him in conversation. He politely declined. If he liked you, he just wanted to be near you, but he didn't want to impose anything more than his simple presence. He reminded me of a monk. Louis repeatedly asked Mr. Hall to be his teacher, until one day in the library Mr. Hall raised his voice to an impressive bellow as he tried to help Louis understand that teachers are everywhere in life and that the world is our teacher. Louis bowed his head to Mr. Hall. We never saw him again.

In the PRS mail room a guy by the name of Steven Ross smiled over the Xerox machine while he made copies of obscure lectures and piles of books. It turned out that Steven had not so long ago been a candidate for successor to Mr. Hall, despite his lack of any desire for the gig. When he heard about Ronnie assisting Marie he smiled wryly, mentioning he had narrowly avoided the same fate. From what I could tell, Steven had no personal life at all. I once told him during a phone conversation that he sounded like a voice detached from the physical body. He responded, "When you say 'I' and you don't mean your body because you have a body but you are not your body, then you're well on your way along the path." Always researching, advising someone, or helping someone in need, here was the kind of guy who could get tears in his eyes when the breeze was just right with the sun shining on his face, as he sincerely exemplified a deeply spiritual appreciation for life and being in the moment. I'm still convinced when he got home he probably took his body off and hung it up in the closet on a wooden hanger.

We asked Steven what brought him to PRS. A dream. Dreams had been guiding him on an epic journey to gather information from all around the world about alternative and unusual methods of healing involving color, electricity, herbs, elixirs, the recipes of medieval sages like Paracelsus, and the advice of psychics like Edgar Cayce. In turn, Steven asked us what brought us to PRS and Ronnie explained the earthquake anxiety that Mr. Hall addressed in that first lecture. Steven smiled and asked, "As if he was talking right at you?" It had happened to Steven too, and according to him many others. Steven believed that Mr. Hall channeled his lectures.

But Mr. Hall had taught us that channeling, or psychic mediumship, was a pitfall. He went Old Testament on it. After all, it's necromancy, trafficking with the dead. Mr. Hall didn't think it was healthy for the medium or the client.

Then Steven invited us to a presentation by the Seer of the Sunbelt, a sleeping prophet popular in the southwest, who would be answering questions about earth changes. We were taken aback. But Steven persisted. And then he offered us the challenge of a free reading. We would not have to meet or communicate in any way with said psychic. We would simply agree to sit quietly for fifteen minutes at a certain time at the address of our choice. Cassettes would arrive in the mail; what did we have to lose? Ronnie and I decided that since Mr. Hall had no reservations about Edgar Cayce, and he had been a friend of his son Hugh Lynn Cayce, we should give it a chance.

This was before the internet so you couldn't whip up a scam so easily. Steven didn't know any details about our lives. Our conversations were rarely personal. But then the cassettes arrived. Despite a Scottish accent that was very difficult to understand, the voice on the cassette knew more about Ronnie and me than our parents, our closest friends, even ourselves. How in the hell did this total stranger know things no one else could possibly know? Where did he get the information? We decided to attend the seminar about earth changes at a Ramada Inn in Chatsworth. I was nervous. If there was a relapse of Edgar Cayce's "Earth Changes" fever, I'd be moving to Virginia Beach faster than you can say San Andreas.

The Reverend Edward A. Monroe was a salt of the earth older man with a gentle demeanor and an unpretentious calm, but a WWII squint. His readings had no attributes of theater. No lighting effects or costumes. Not even a hint of sage in the air, and he wasn't Scottish like the voice on the cassette, he was half Cherokee. A great North American dad through and through, he was one of the kindest men I've ever met. He didn't need smudge because he had the white light of the Christ, he would say.

Ed reclined in a chair. A tape recorder played "Amazing Grace" on bagpipes. His breathing became deep and steady. The room became very still. The voice we had heard on tape spoke through Ed. That Scottish spirit, named Jock, was allegedly a regimental surgeon from back in the 1800s, very well read, with a sharp wit, but a brogue that was thick as porridge. The session began with Jock saying what would become a familiar refrain: "Aye, yes, indeed, it seems the laddie is properly gone now."

Jock's lecture had the same wholesome quality as Mr. Hall's. They certainly had the same commonsense approach to living a better life.

As for fear of earthquakes, Jock said that human beings are always looking for punishment; that examining the psychological basis of our fears would do more good than speculating about the dates of natural disasters that might still be modified by the choices societies and individuals make. Jock suggested that perhaps Cayce's earth change predictions had not happened as predicted because society had evolved significantly. He pointed to the increasing popularity of ideas like reincarnation, astrology, and self-help, as signs of a more soulful approach to living. We eagerly told the Halls about our experience, and they were not in the least skeptical or disapproving, but they were completely uninterested in a free reading.

Steven soon left PRS to start a nonprofit organization, the World Research Foundation. He would travel the world, from Bali to Beijing and all points in between. His dreams took him a long way. Having devoted his life to preserving the books and inventions of forgotten geniuses, from legendary microscopes to ancient manuals of dream interpretation, his library in Sedona is like a small PRS.

Meanwhile, we became friends with Ed and with Jock, two very different men, both father figures I miss to this day. The first time I had a reading in person I was nervous. Confronted by this new personality in the room I wondered how one is supposed to talk to the dead? "So, hi," I ventured. He laughed. "Hi lass. Do you have a question?" "Yes, I do. Before we get started with all this, so, you're dead, right?" "Aye, yes indeed." "Because you're dead you can see not only my present life now but you can also see my past lives and my possible lives in the future, right? You can see everything about my life?" "Yes, lass, we do our best." "Well, since there's no secrets here I might as well get comfortable." I took off my shoes and picked up my list of questions. The conversation those questions started lasted ten years.

Ed once told me the story of how he became a trance channel. Bored with the aimlessness of retirement, after his long career as a car mechanic with the Los Angeles Police Department, he had taken a road trip to think things through. He stopped at the Church of the

Red Rocks in Sedona, Arizona. No one was around. The door was open. He went inside, sat down, and began to pray. He wanted to be of service. He was willing to do anything to be useful. But the anything that emerged was not what he expected. I think that "no good deed goes unpunished" phrase goes with what happened next.

After several incidents of finding that he had driven to the parking lot of a certain hypnotist, without having any memory of having done so, Ed decided to go inside. Wondering if he was losing his mind, he let the hypnotist induce a trance. Ed woke up to find the hypnotist looking at him with an astonished expression, holding a pad full of notes. The hypnotist informed Ed that a spirit had spoken through him and left instructions and explanations. When Ed protested that he could not tolerate Jock giving medical advice, he began seeing, as if projected on a wall, the names and phone numbers of people the day before they called him.

But Ed was spiritual in his own way without Jock. Once a scrub jay adopted him. Whenever Ed would get in the car to drive into Taos, the blue bird followed him all the way to town. The jay would wait by his car, then fly alongside for the ride home.

Cats and dogs liked to curl up on Ed when he went to sleep to channel. Once Ed sent a client their cassette, only to be told that a mooing cow had commandeered the audio. Next session Ed had a lookout. Sure enough, the neighbor's cow sashayed over from her pasture. She looked in the window and began mooing.

An example of Ed's psychic sensitivity, and of his kindness, happened when one of my felines passed. At the market buying food for the other cats I felt deep grief, and for a moment the tears flowed under the buzz of florescent light. When I got home, as I opened the door, the phone started ringing. Ed said he recognized my perfume and felt I was crying. He knew something was wrong and wanted to make sure I was okay.

Mr. Hall offered choices, parables, and context. Jock challenged my fears, my beliefs, and disbeliefs. He identified the spots where my profound stubbornness truly held me back, limiting my experience of the world and of the spiritual side of life. With Jock I felt free to question the universe and what it's doing out there. He always had great answers. I loved Ed. But I had life-changing talks with Jock. The dead guy understood me better than anyone else I had ever spoken to in my life.

When Ed came to LA on a visit from Taos he had many readings set up. They usually happened in a Mission Revival one-story house with a backyard of mature apricot trees in the San Fernando Valley. The place belonged to a gay couple. Victor was a past-life-regression therapist. George was sly, dry, and spry. He had been an organist with a traveling circus. He had channeled material he wanted to make into a book, so Ronnie and a couple of George's other friends edited what eventually became *The Writings of the Mantira-Book 1*. The book begins with the statement: "These writings are for those of you who once lived in a certain time and area of this planet. Their purpose is to reawaken in you the spiritual properties that were highly developed and much used in that place and period." George also published a book of Spiritualist devotional poems called *My Lord, You Are Magic*.

Victor made heavenly apricot preserves. He would send us home with bags heavy with jars of it. We'd bring back the empties for replacements. Victor not only looked like a monk, he laughed like one with the clear peal of a bell in his voice. From vows of silence to the longest fasts I ever witnessed, Victor must have been a monk somewhere else besides the Renaissance Faire that we went to together. He would invite us over for dinner to feed us homemade breads and soups with generously poured glasses of sherry.

We shared many meals with Victor and George at the Siamese Princess Restaurant on Third Street in Hollywood, a place Ronnie had first taken me to when it was a hole-in-the-wall with six tables in a strip mall adjacent to a gas station. The new location had walls covered with portraits of Thai royalty but also Princess Diana, and for décor there were elaborate Thai carvings and lavish flower arrangements. That's the place where we would have our wedding reception, with the Halls in attendance.

Around that time Ronnie had difficulty shaking a case of the flu, so the Halls took us to one of their favorite doctors, a chiropractor, except he wouldn't be adjusting Ronnie's back. Instead, he'd use a special diagnostic tool of his own invention. Marie drove us into Beechwood Canyon to meet Dr. Sabia and his Electro Stimulating Machine. An improbable contraption in the form of a huge wooden rectangle, it took up most of the wall in the small front room of a shady old Hollywood Hills house overgrown with foliage and covered by fallen leaves.

The Electro Stimulating Machine looked like it was designed by Rube Goldberg. Sabia put a nickel plate in Ronnie's one hand and a copper plate in the other. I was standing by with folded arms. It's probably a good thing no one saw the expression on my face. Were they going to electrocute Ronnie? Sabia was an intense old guy moving quickly, working all thirty-five of the machine's big dials as Mr. and Mrs. Hall looked on approvingly. Sabia claimed he was reading the frequencies of Ronnie's organs. I thought most of his diagnosis common sense. After Jock's accurate descriptions of precisely which vertebrae needed adjusting, we were hard to impress.

Each scenario played out like a fable. Louis found out his calling was out in the world, not sitting at someone's feet being instructed. Steven collected every form of healing he could possibly find to share with the world. Marianne gave comfort to the dying, inspiration to the living, and later ran for president. Ed and Jock brought spiritualism to many Christian retirees. Victor and George left Los Angeles, taking with them their house and the old apricot trees.

THE PINCH HITTER

The 3:00 p.m. routine. Mr. Hall would have his afternoon libation, a coffee and a cookie. Only that wasn't always coffee in his cup; sometimes it was a double gin martini, or so Edith would have us believe. Ronnie and I would meet up in Edith's office where she'd inspect my baking while questioning both of us about what we'd been up to that day. Ronnie always had some revelation to share. Soon she would guide us into Mr. Hall's office to include him in the conversation and give him his strictly rationed extra cookie. For me this meant I could resume my ongoing altar investigation.

Then came that fateful afternoon in Edith's office when she challenged Ronnie to give a lecture. Her co-conspirator, Pearl, stood in the doorway smiling. Pearl was in junior high the first time her mother brought her to a lecture by Mr. Hall. She had grown up at PRS. She put on the glasses that hung from a chain around her neck, put up her chin, and smiled at Ronnie. What a wonderful idea, she agreed.

Ronnie didn't want to lecture. Too much opportunity for embarrassment. I told him he should talk to Mr. Hall about it, so we called and were invited over. Mr. Hall was sitting under the double tree. Ronnie joined him there. I helped Marie make a meal in the kitchen, following her around like a puppy. She told me stories about her childhood, before the war changed everything.

On the drive home I found out what Mr. Hall had told Ronnie. He should lecture. He should not use notes. If he didn't know his subject well enough to lecture without them, he shouldn't lecture at all. Ronnie also had several beautiful Chinese silk ties that Mr. Hall had given him from his own collection. He had also taken the time to teach Ronnie how to tie a Windsor knot.

Not only did Pearl book Ronnie a lecture, she gave him a Sunday morning, the spotlight slot usually reserved for Mr. Hall, or veteran metaphysical teachers such as Dr. Stephan Hoeller, a Jungian Gnostic Bishop, and Roger Weir, founder of Whirling Rainbow Institute, or another prominent special guest. Never for an unknown. Ronnie, beside himself with nerves, showed great dedication, carefully preparing and steadying himself for a ninety-minute lecture without notes. His parents were all over him because he was going to humiliate them with his failure.

The only time I saw Ronnie get flustered that day was when, despite Mr. Hall's tutorial, he could not get that Windsor knot right. I drove him to his first lecture. The parking lot was full but this time we drove right up and the orange cone was moved aside so we could park in the spot reserved for Mr. Hall.

The packed house was buzzing. Who was this kid that the old man has been hanging around with so much? From my point of view this was a definitive moment, as Ronnie attempted to demonstrate the alchemical transmutation before my eyes. The guy I had met not long before was a pathological liar motivated by his worst instincts. A bad boy whose life was a kind of road rage. More reaction than thought. The Ronnie I had first known was at rock bottom. A singer who lost his band. A rabble rouser who had lost his rabble. A heavy drinker who never got drunk. Cereal and White Russians at dusk is not a good breakfast for a twenty-year-old. That was the guy getting up there on stage standing at the lectern near Mr. Hall's big chair.

Just before Ronnie took the stage Arthur offered to fix his tie. He seemed impressed when Ronnie told him it was a gift from Mr. Hall. I took a seat in the audience next to Ronnie's nervous parents. Ronnie walked onto the stage with a surprisingly calm expression and a slight smile. He stood with angular grace. Despite a short haircut he still had the unruly curly hair of a poet. He gave a detailed, well-organized, inspiring lecture about New England Transcendentalism, with a few laughs in the right spots. He had paid attention to Mr. Hall's Sunday lectures and delivered his version. People started taking notes. Nodding along. Exchanging impressed glances. Quite a transition from the guy with the black cigarette in the rain.

When Ronnie finished, the crowd applauded its approval. The old timers were delighted to see this new arrival. Younger people were stunned to see one of their own. Ronnie had to shake a lot of hands and hear a lot of accolades. From then on the lady who made flower arrangements for Mr. Hall brought bouquets for Ronnie's lectures, too. Edith and Pearl looked like the proverbial cats that ate the canaries. Edith nicknamed Ronnie the Great Synthesizer.

Mr. Hall seemed pleased by reports of Ronnie's success. At his advanced age, Mr. Hall sometimes didn't feel up to lecturing. At first these lapses were infrequent. Hoeller and Weir were both seasoned lecturers. They had substituted for Mr. Hall many times and were more than qualified. But Mr. Hall asked Ronnie to be his backup. Any lecture Mr. Hall had to miss, Ronnie would give. Naturally, the first lecture as designated substitute was more than just a little intimidating.

The audience expected to see Mr. Hall and some were not thrilled at this decidedly young stranger. Ronnie delivered another flawless performance. Then another. And another. It was spooky. I don't know what he was tapping into, but the tap was good. That, and the fact that Mr. Hall had chosen him as official substitute, was taken by some of the regulars as an indication that the rumors about a successor might be true. Was that initiate fever I began sensing from some in the crowd? A few of them were downright giddy, too excited, their enthusiasm had an air of desperation.

Not everyone was happy about Ronnie's success. Pat wanted PRS to have legitimacy and sustainability. Ronnie didn't even have a bachelor's degree. Factions were offended by Ronnie's quick promotion. He worked so closely with Mr. Hall at this point, helping go through his mail and answering letters on his behalf, that several people who had been there much longer and had little access felt slighted. No matter, Ronnie was now booked to deliver a series of weekly lectures in the room upstairs, off the library, where the portrait of Madame Blavatsky would peer down from behind him as he lectured.

It wasn't long before Ronnie's Friday and Saturday lectures got a special mention in the *PRS Journal,* in Pearl's column *Happenings at Headquarters.* We were even given the key to the library. Before Ronnie's lectures we wandered hand in hand, exploring the treasures, with no one else there to disturb us. Every night we made sure to shut off the lights when we left.

Suddenly, Ronnie and I were surrounded by people bent on manipulating what they thought was the heir apparent. I found them daunting since I had barely graduated high school. I was an undiagnosed dyslexic. These people had degrees and years of specialized study. Some had traveled around the world. I collected fairy tale books. I was out of my league. My new status as girlfriend of the boy genius left a lot to be desired. The men were very dismissive of me. I was supposed to say thank you and you're welcome and nothing else, or I would be thought intrusive. The women at best were condescending and eager to demonstrate intellectual prowess. At worst they were as dismissive as the men and excited to find out that Ronnie and I were not married. They didn't bother to hide their predatory smiles when I said we weren't. Sometimes I'd make eye contact with Ronnie and he'd lip-read me saying "incoming" as one of these mavens of metaphysics approached him.

WARNINGS
FROM THE SYBILS

As Ronnie's lectures gained popularity, occasional newcomers began fawning on me. Some were lovely people delighted to make my acquaintance and exchange ideas. But at least one woman at every lecture would take me aside to tell me about how lucky I was to be in the presence of the young genius and the old master. Of course, their aim was to use me as a go-between. They wanted Ronnie to tell them all about their destinies. Also, Ronnie was just one step from Manly Hall. To use their terminology, their astral agendas cloyed my auric field. They were in it to win it in a most unseemly fashion.

I wasn't sure how best to navigate the fact that such a nervous boy with such a rough start should be seen by so many people as a source of wisdom. On the other hand, he was spending every day studying what he was lecturing about and making wonderful discoveries enlightening not only to himself. Even established scholars often learned something new at his lectures. Mr. Hall trusted Ronnie's research.

Meanwhile, everything Ronnie studied I studied too. This spiritual journey we took very seriously and no detail went unexamined. We were meditating daily. We were learning how to feed not only mind but body. We were applying the principles in our lives. After the lectures, back home with important visitors, my job was to make things pleasant while the men had discussions. And the useless bullshit they talked about could have filled volumes and libraries, and in fact they do. Most of these philosophical giants couldn't heat a can of soup in a pan. These conversations had the urgency of Marie's utopian manias, but at least she could make a good dinner. Any time I'd get irritated, I'd be told I wasn't being spiritual enough. One of these jackasses put out a cigarette on my carpet and I wasn't allowed to say anything because "the men were talking."

Then began the dark warnings. After one of Ronnie's lectures, out of nowhere, Peggy, the astrologer Mr. Hall had chosen for us, took me aside in the cool stillness of the dimly-lit library after closing time. She had always been chatty and gregarious with me but now she turned with narrowed eyes and the ominous tone of an unhappy divorcee: "Don't live through a man," she said. "You'll regret it if you do." Unfortunately, she did not take her own good advice.

Before long Peggy succumbed to the compulsion suffered by her patients. She was a shadow of her former self the last time I saw her. Ronnie spoke with her about it. He reminded her of what she had told me. She dismissed him as hopelessly naive. What could he know about facing life alone as an older woman? He didn't even appreciate that his relationship with me was one of the causes of her preoccupation with marriage. Soon she wasn't visiting PRS as often as she had. We later heard that she died on the operating table during plastic surgery.

Through the open door to Mr. Hall's office I listened as Ronnie asked for guidance about how to handle desperate people. I sat across from Edith in her office and remarked: "Most of them need a shrink, not a spiritual advisor." Edith gave me that same look Peggy did. She had seen what happened to the Halls as Manly's following soured on Marie. If I spoke up too much or showed any hint of a disagreeable nature, Edith warned me how easily I could be branded a "Mad Marie."

Then the Great Sybil took me aside, "Mad Marie" herself. In her kitchen she put me in a corner to sit and smoke a cigarette, despite which I felt as if I was in a high chair being scolded by my German grandma. She told me not to let Ronnie go along the same path that

Papa did. The path of male dominant ego, patriarchal brainwashing, idolatry. I had to speak my own truth and be my own person. When Marie met Manly he was too far gone, she said. A world-famous writer and lecturer touring the big cities. But she thought with Ronnie I still had a chance. If I could be myself, maybe he could be himself. Only when the genders are equal can there be enlightenment. I realized that kitchen was the lab of an alchemist, and I was one of her experiments.

BOOK HUNTING
WITH THE HALLS

Edith and Mr. Hall decided Ronnie was college material. To my surprise Ronnie took up the challenge. He was highly aware that Mr. Hall had been dismissed by academia. He would become the old man's champion. He would defend his mentor and the entire fields of astrology and metaphysics, using the tools of academia against the prejudices of the professors. He wanted to give legitimacy to PRS. Ronnie's insistence that he go over each day's learning with me meant we got two college educations for the price of one. It worked out well for Ronnie, too. He learned everything so well he stopped studying. He just paid close attention the day of the lesson, then taught it to me. He aced all his tests and graduated from Occidental College in record time.

That summer Ronnie took a part-time job in a used bookstore in West Hollywood, called Canterbury Books, run by a salty old character with the appropriate name of Charlie Saltzman. I started going to PRS less, since Ronnie wasn't there as much, so I had more time on my hands. Instead of his pay, one month Ronnie showed up with the Julian Editions ten-volume set, *The Complete Works of Percy Bysshe Shelley,* in beautiful green cloth with white vellum spines and black and gilt leather labels. I found them hypnotic. That was my summer of reading Shelley.

It fascinated me to read the poems, then to read Mary Shelley's notes about them. "The Sensitive Plant" made me cry. I recognized the ideas of Plotinus in "Hymn to Intellectual Beauty." *Prometheus Unbound* un-bound my mind. I think what I loved most about Shelley were his gorgeous and almost supernaturally accurate descriptions of nature. But once I read about what jerks he and most of the other English Romantics were, my passion for his art cooled. I think Keats was the only good egg in the entire coop.

At one of our dinners with the Halls, Ronnie dared talk about interesting books he had found in the used bookstores of Los Angeles. Marie told him not to waste his time, but he piqued her interest when he mentioned that one store had a reprint of *The Wither's Booke,* an old emblem book used for divination, dating from the era of Francis Bacon. *The Wither's Booke* had been key to Marie's work.

Mr. Hall encouraged Ronnie to pick out books for the library to consider. When he came up with some good choices and interesting finds, Marie thought this was a good opportunity for Papa to get some exercise. It would be good for him to get out and about. Marie took the wheel for our visit to three bookstores Ronnie had chosen. As I mentioned before, Marie got us there in record time, and as always it was thrilling.

At Dailey's Book Shop, Mr. Hall was welcomed enthusiastically by William Dailey, who had set up a comfortable chair in the middle of his store. Bill brought Mr. Hall books to inspect; several were acquired by the library. After examining a book himself, Mr. Hall would hand it to Marie; she had to approve. We got to look over the books, too, as she handed them to us. These were some nice antiquarian finds, including a beautiful copy of a rare book by Robert Fludd.

At the next two stores the stairs denied Mr. Hall access, so the Halls waited in the car while Ronnie fetched the owners. After a respectful handshake, books were shown curbside. At one store the owner produced his personal copy of *The Secret Teachings of All Ages,* which was then inscribed for him by the author. MPH directed several choice but affordable books our way, including a copy of *The Secret Symbols of the*

Rosicrucians that contained parchment prints of complicated charts, many with concentric circles that reminded us of Marie's mystical diagrams.

After a couple more bookstore expeditions in the weeks that followed, Marie came up with a better idea, because now all Mr. Hall was doing was sitting in the car instead of walking, a kind of bibliophile drive-through. He was bringing home more of those dusty old books she had so little tolerance for. The *Nepalese Ragamala Album and Gilt Bronzes Exhibit* at the Norton Simon Museum had attracted her attention. Marie proposed an excursion. Asian art with the Halls? That was the beckoning cat's meow as far as I was concerned.

On a lovely weekday afternoon we survived another brisk drive with Marie. We all walked together through the exhibit, slowly, because Mr. Hall moved slowly; the ideal pace for viewing sacred treasures. We listened to the Halls' comments about the art. They shared historical facts related to the objects. They explained uses of color or lack thereof, revealing symbolism or peculiarities of time and place. Mr. Hall said something about a piece. Marie corrected him. Usually their differences involved interpreting the meaning of a detail. Ronnie and I listened carefully as these two connoisseurs bantered. A pair of encyclopedias conversing right in front of us.

We walked into an anteroom featuring a spot-lit sculpture: a life-size stone Bodhisattva Maitreya from Ancient Gandhara, nineteen hundred years young. Mr. Hall stood to the right of it with Marie. As I walked up, impressed by its beauty, I stopped in my tracks. I looked at Mr. Hall like a dog that had just seen a card trick. I looked back at the statue. I looked back at Mr. Hall. He and that statue looked a lot alike. Marie snickered. Mr. Hall gave me the Groucho-style raised eyebrows. He chuckled. Marie quipped, "You're more handsome in this life anyway." She smiled at him with that "I'm sweet on you" look in her eyes. That happened quite a bit, when she'd call him her Canadian Bacon, referring to Sir Francis. Or when she'd correct his posture by saying, "Papa, stop shtupping," with no idea of the double entendre.

Marie's continuing efforts to get Mr. Hall to get some fresh air ended abruptly. He happily sank back into his comfortable routine. However, her efforts would soon be revived again, coupled this time with ambition, which required attending out-of-state events featuring her work. Mr. Hall would have to face the physical ordeals of travel, including road trips in an RV. But we were long gone by then.

MIDNIGHT ARCHAEOLOGY

Marie never talked with us about working in the movie business, though allegedly she worked as an extra in more than a dozen films. For a long time we didn't know that there had been a first Mrs. Hall, who had ended her own life. We also didn't know that Marie had suffered a series of breakdowns that caused her first husband to institutionalize her, probably only reinforcing her PTSD. We had no idea she was suffering from blood sugar spikes, but then again neither did she. She found out long after we were gone. To us Marie just seemed high strung, a bit over zealous, and indulged by Mr. Hall.

Marie's mission had begun in the 1940s with a vision of Abraham Lincoln. She claimed he walked into the room looking as solid as you or me. He told her she had a special destiny related to the fate of America. A long series of unlikely coincidences involving anagrams and secret codes led her to the conviction that a certain grave, the Bruton Vault in Colonial Williamsburg, Virginia, contained the original Shakespeare plays, each in the handwriting of none other than Sir Francis Bacon. There too would be found documents instrumental in every major development of Western civilization including the discovery and evolution of America. Best of all, she believed, scientific breakthroughs would be found there that could not be given to the world back then. But now they would be. They would end all sickness and want.

Marie traumatized the town of Williamsburg with her midnight archaeology. Controversy ensued. The year of Kristallnacht in Germany, one year before WWII began, there she was on local radio, appealing to destiny and hurling accusations of conspiracy in her thick German accent. Marie upset the locals. I know she traumatized the town because a friend of mine, Paul Johnson, was a young man there when it happened. He grew up to be a scholar who wrote important academic books on Edgar Cayce and Madame Blavatsky's mysterious masters. Knowing Marie, she might try to take credit for the inspiration she bestowed.

Undaunted, Marie began her decades-long quest to advance her work so as to save humanity. She showed a report of a test that indicated copper cylinders in the ground where she said they'd be. Others called it an anomaly. A later test that revealed no hidden treasure she dismissed as manipulation by the Rockefellers, who were in charge of the renovation of the historic site. At first, the vestry assisted her. Bemused by her cryptic evidence and enthusiasm, they used their own workers to begin the dig. But then suddenly changed their minds. What happened to change their minds?

Marie believed that most likely the Rockefellers had used underground tunnels to take away these great gifts to humanity. Therefore it would require the *vox populi,* the voice of the people, to demand the return of their heritage, of their rightful bequest from Francis Bacon and his fellow visionaries. I must admit I didn't get it, no matter how many times she told me I did. The types I grew up around didn't give a damn about Shakespeare, but they did like bacon.

Hidden secrets are the stuff of which the history of metaphysics is made. All over the world there are examples of entombed wisdom. From Howard Carter's looting of Tut's burial chamber, to those Rosicrucians who allegedly found the vault where the body of Christian Rosenkreutz lay intact after hundreds of years; they touched nothing and closed it up again, but learned from what they had seen. Marie's vault contained secret teachings that would benefit all humanity, not only the few. Her vault was so much more illustrious and mysterious than Mr. Hall's, don't you know.

"What about the little guy?" Marie often asked Mr. Hall. "For most people working their jobs and just trying to get by, what are all those books going to do for them?" She never seemed to see the irony that her books were the only exception. Instead she'd criticize him and his methods. Papa had the brain power, the good looks, the inclination, the success, the self-infatuation that men have. Mr. Hall pretended to be hurt by her insult, making her laugh, most of the time. If she didn't laugh we all knew we were in for it. On those occasions her criticism of him could bring him to tears, and us, too, as she denied that he ever really achieved anything, he was just taking advantage of gullible people. She had originated a new vision of the universe. All he had done was repeat old ideas.

Now I must admit I never got how the revelations that Francis Bacon really wrote the Shakespeare plays and America was a Rosicrucian invention would somehow bring enlightenment to the masses. But Marie imagined that they would be moved by the compassion of Bacon and his cohorts. Somehow the national conscience would awaken into an enlightened society where women would take their rightful place alongside men. Sometimes Marie's eyes welled up with joyful tears as she described the Space Mother, or she raised her fist with indignation at those who deliberately kept the common folk in poverty and ignorance. She had little patience for what she called "Trial and Error Democracy." Her eyes flashed as she shook her jewelry like a shaman.

I witnessed a somewhat awkward meeting between Marie and groundbreaking author Jean Houston. Jean seemed to be fascinated by Marie's personalized view of mythology, but Marie wasn't comfortable having what she considered her great revelation of the Truth with a capital T included in the collection of world myths. I remember Jean smiling and saying: "Well, what is a meta for?" A comment followed by a moment of uncomfortable silence. I believe Marie could have benefited from Jean's comprehensive and inclusive perspective. They had much in common. But Marie's messianic preoccupation made it almost impossible for her to recognize the value of peers.

Now I could not know it at the time but Marie Bauer Hall was actually the first riot grrrl I ever met. It would be ten years before I'd meet Kathleen Hanna. But in retrospect it's clear to me that Marie was a card-carrying representative of riot grrrl, from the tips of her platform shoes to her rough shorn black curls.

"What is riot grrrl," you ask? Well, even if you didn't, I'm going to tell you. Riot grrrl had its heyday in the 1990s when feminists in the indie punk music world formed our own scene. Bands, handmade pamphlets called zines, riot grrrl chapters, and online chat rooms had sprung up all over America, the UK, and a few other parts of the world.

Was Marie a riot grrrl? Well, you tell me. Here's the list, let's see: self-published paper booklets and books with titles like *Common Sense and the Battle of the Sexes*? Check. Sometimes indecipherable run-on sentences and complicated cut-up diagrams and illustrations made of elements lifted from all sorts of otherwise unrelated sources? Check. Rants about history, patriarchy, and injustice? Check. A utopian vision of a society based on equality? Check. Irritation at the indignities of gender discrimination? Check. Rape survivor, got pregnant, had to abort? Check. Check. Check. Trying to organize a grassroots movement of the people to wake up the masses? Check. Untreated PTSD? Check. Dismissed as loud, mentally unstable, and prone to bouts of hysteria? Checkmate. If Marie Hall had been born sixty years later and went to Evergreen College in Olympia, Washington, she probably would have started a riot grrrl chapter, a zine, and her own band.

Marie wrote letters to American presidents and world leaders, offering her prescription for a new order of peace and enlightenment. With the help of her most loyal supporter, Fred Cole, she did everything she could to spread her word. Fred was a quiet chap, so dedicated to Marie he once took a job as a janitor in DC so he could deliver messages from her to the leaders of the nation. To me Fred seemed like a good-natured granddad who ought to be cultivating a lovely garden, but he believed Marie's revelation without reservation. Marie wrote J. Edgar Hoover and the FBI so much she earned a condemnation any riot grrrl would be proud of: Public Nuisance.

In Marie's feminist metaphysics, Zeus and Jesus co-exist with the Space Mother. But these were symbols, she continually reminded us, not to be taken literally. Marie tried to map not only consciousness but creation in a series of huge diagrams of great symmetrical beauty. As she opened these mighty scrolls on a drawing board in her office, I felt like I was seeing blueprints of consciousness. One, she claimed, displayed the geometry of the Garden of Eden in a mandala of metaphors.

She was told she was lucky to have survived the war, whatever may have happened. Told to find her purpose in motherhood and house-keeping. Then, a chance meeting at a train station: A gentleman told her that instead of waiting around for her delayed train, she should go listen to Manly Palmer Hall lecture at a nearby venue. So she did. After the lecture Mr. Hall found her in the crowd and advised her to study metaphysics. The revelations that followed gave her a new passion for life, but got in the way of housework and raising children. Uprooting her household and moving to Los Angeles to be near PRS still didn't satisfy. Marie gathered up her research, left her family, and devoted her-self fully to her new mission. When she first met Manly, she told me, she could see right away that he needed her "to bring him back down to earth."

I believe with Mr. Hall she found a co-conspirator and one of the best enablers ever. He acquired rare books for her that she needed to continue her studies. He brought her talented assistants to help her make her vision a reality, or at least keep her busy for a while. But she thought that her husband should use his pulpit to preach her gospel.

Sometimes it felt like Ronnie, Mr. Hall, and I were dim-witted stu-dents in her living room class. Once Mr. Hall volunteered to give a lec-ture on her philosophy despite the warnings of Edith and others who reminded the old man that such a lecture could go very south very fast, and indeed had in the past. It did this time as well.

Sitting between Ronnie and me at the lecture Marie squirmed with impatience, and like a real riot grrrl she heckled and corrected Mr. Hall. Everything he said was wrong. Mr. Hall never wavered. He soldiered on like a trooper. Marie never seemed to notice the annoyed audience members glancing at her or their many shushes and ahems.

Marie had an epic Teutonic tantrum back in Mr. Hall's office, on the ride home, and then for a couple more hours in the living room. She even whipped up dinner while bitching the entire time. Ronnie endured the brunt of her Wagnerian outrage while Mr. Hall and I bravely retreated to self-induced catatonia; it was our only defense. You could hear *Ride of the Valkyries* in that woman's voice. Ronnie explained that Mr. Hall had tried to translate her work into a language that his audience could understand. She was having none of it.

Ronnie suggested perhaps she should lecture on her own work. I looked at Mr. Hall. He had that "my headache just got worse" expression. "I get too excited," she said, waving Ronnie off. Ronnie finally calmed her down when he agreed to give a lecture on her work with her coaching. And so Ronnie quelled the storm and, as far as Mr. Hall was concerned, Ronnie was the new official go-to for dealing with Marie. That was not fair. But at least she paid him. Ronnie's lecture about Marie's work was a success, though the community remained skeptical of "Mad Marie." Best of all, Marie trusted Ronnie enough not to attend.

When we earnestly asked Mr. Hall what he thought of Marie's philosophy he told us he believed that she was most probably an outsider visionary in the tradition of mystics like Jacob Boehme. As for the Bruton Vault, Mr. Hall had written that, when in Europe, Benjamin Franklin worked with St. Germain on the invention of the American nation. Husband and wife had more in common than not. Certainly, it would appear, that his mission kindled hers.

THE SPACE MOTHER

I heard a lot about the Space Mother Principle. Marie told me I intuitively, down to my DNA, got what she meant. After hours of explanations, charts, statistics, graphics, I felt like I was under hypnotic trance. Two hours into it Marie hadn't taken a breath. It looked like Mr. Hall had been snoozing for an hour, and I had a headache. Marie paused to ask Mr. Hall if he knew a certain date. Eyes still closed he was right there with it. I thought the old boy had nodded off.

By the end of her stream of consciousness, I felt groggy from a non-stop utopian Germanic monologue. Ronnie seemed to be following her theory. He surprised her by asking questions that I didn't understand. Her beaming smile lit the room. "You see, Manly, he gets it! He's young, he doesn't need those dusty books!" Mr. Hall glanced at me with a comical expression of sorrow, which of course made me laugh. "Oh, Papa!" Marie scolded Mr. Hall. As always, our reward for our patience was dessert.

Marie talked about the Space Mother Principle with great affection. Like Marie, the Space Mother remained unknown despite offering salvation for all. Because the Space Mother was the source of all creation, enlightenment had to be inevitable. "People will wake up," she'd smile with animated conviction. "I'll bet you dollars to donuts."

What was Marie's Space Mother? The goddess behind all the other gods and goddesses, the one that gave them being and place. Her infinite love allows them to forget her. Marie was moved by that forgetting and by the selfless love of the Space Mother willing to be forgotten. Infatuated with power, certain gods forgot the Space Mother. The creations of their amnesia trap souls in bodies. As above so below; when the gods forget we all forget, and that is how we human beings forgot our true natures.

For Marie the second coming of Christ was nothing less than the awakening of the higher consciousness in every single human being. Her eyes welled up with tears as she described the grace and the grandeur, the billions of infinitely merciful hands of the bodhisattva Avalokiteshvara.

Marie practiced a unique form of astrology. Her mythological approach gave the planets souls and personalities. The planet Jupiter is no mere gaseous giant named after an ancient Roman deity. As far as Marie was concerned the Romans had rebranded the ancient Greek ruler of the gods Zeus. The planet Jupiter, then, is the vehicle of Zeus in the ongoing evolution of civilization. By understanding how celestial Jupiter has interacted with humanity throughout history an astrologer can see the actual will of Zeus in action.

Marie used Roman numerals to explain how consciousness divides into matter, a complicated process involving vibrations, angles, directions, and dimensions. I was touched by her view of time as a merciful law of the universe, eternity's power of creating imaginary divisions and measures to allow even the humblest beings to evolve. She pointed out that she never wore a watch. "I have too much respect for time to wear it on my wrist."

Right about now you may be wondering how I remember so much detail about Marie's beliefs after I said I didn't get it. Repetition, my dear reader, repetition.

Central to her mission was the Universal Reformation as understood by the Rosicrucians. However, Marie's Universal Reformation was a truly equal society of plenty where no one would horde while others lacked.

A world where women, with our soulful understanding of life, would wake humanity from the nightmare of history.

Marie took initiate fever to a different level. Perhaps it's best explained in her own words:

> Whether or not we have recognized them, or appreciated them as such, throughout immature microcosmic Soul and Family-history on Earth and in Time, solar enlightened, and soul-enlightened members of either our own macrocosmic Solar Family system, or "relatives" and professional members pertaining to other space-studding cosmic-solar Family-systems, perhaps even to "more advanced" and therefore "enlightened" microcosmic offspring of other Solar-Family systems, etc., have periodically become incarnated from among our human earth-generations for specific assignment to a divine-parentally appointed task.

Marie's favorite term for these higher beings from other worlds incarnating into ours to help us was "babysitters." Her Francis Bacon, born the legitimate son of Queen Elizabeth I from her secret marriage with the Earl of Leicester, was the reincarnation of not only Adam but also Saint Peter.

Marie considered the fictional character Dr. Dolittle an esoteric key to the understanding of Francis Bacon's mission. Dolittle had regained Adam's language, and so he could talk to the animals, symbolic of Bacon's many scientific pursuits that allowed nature to speak her secrets.

Marie found reflections of her theories in unlikely places: a patriotic Red Cross poster distributed to American schools during World War II, mysterious marks on Colonial gravestones, a children's movie starring Rex Harrison, and the obscure poetry books *The Testament of Beauty* by Robert Bridges and *The Sonnets of G.S.O.*

Marie unabashedly plundered all religions for her metaphors. The entire world magnified the meaning of her theories. She discovered obscure connections between people who otherwise had nothing in common. Secret messages were revealed to her from anywhere, even billboards and dreams.

In her magnum opus, *Inquiry Into the Nature of Space and of Life in Space,* Marie expressed optimism that it would be the mothers of humanity whose conscience and consciousness would first awaken. She had boundless faith in the power of mothers to change society for the good of their progeny. To Marie all human beings were one family of what she called immature soul collectives. For her the world was a glorious creation of generations of beings incarnate and otherwise, but also an illusion and a pitfall, where the infinite forgets itself in the finite. But divine love shines always. Love is the way to grace. Marie considered herself a Christian, but she was unlike any Christian I had ever met or ever would again. Her father had been a schoolteacher in Germany and a devout Catholic. She laughed that her grandfather's name had been Christian Teufel, meaning Christian Devil. In her philosophy even the most fallen angel could and would be saved; she called this the Christ-Lucifer Reconciliation.

Occasionally, impressionable guests were moved to declare that Marie must indeed be a master like her husband. Marie didn't accept that praise. She pointed out that to be a master you had to have slaves, and she had no interest in slaves, even if they were willing. "We're all in this together," she'd say earnestly.

LOST AND FOUND

One afternoon Ronnie, Pat, Arthur, and several other regulars were engaging in a verbal fencing match, displaying intellectual skills to establish spiritual dominance, as if such a thing were possible. What a bunch of jerks, I thought. Is this going to be my future? An unusually large monarch butterfly fluttered up interrupting the competition for most mystical of the week. It landed on my nose and refused to leave even as I whispered, "Go." Well, everyone knew what that meant symbolically. Ronnie and Arthur smiled at me. The rest skulked away to their separate corners as the conversation ceased. I kept thinking about Peggy's warning.

I got a job at a toy store. This particular toy store was the crown jewel of a glamorous new shopping center. Selling toys was performance art to me. This was improvisation at its finest. Honing in on a child's imagination to find that toy, because finding a toy you love can become a definitive memory from childhood that helps draw the arc of life. I hoped to help each kid find that toy. To see the glee on the child's face and the relief on the parent's face, that was the objective. I rocked the daylights out of retail during my time there. I sold the unsellable seven-hundred-dollar teddy bear. Retail was a relief after PRS. Crying children were easier to deal with than metaphysicians on a mission.

Oddly enough, the store attracted an eerily steady stream of brittle older ladies anxiously asking for Madame Alexander dolls, as if finding one would be a triumph. Both the ladies and the dolls seemed like they belonged in a David Lynch film. Ghosts of another era. We didn't carry those dolls. Their excitement thwarted, they would turn a sneer on me. What kind of person would work at a store that didn't carry Madame Alexander dolls? They reminded me of some of the elitist metaphysicians I had met who seemed to think only they knew what was of true value.

One fateful day a new shipment of stock arrived. I saw a classic Steiff teddy with a hint of koala around the ears, pure adorability. I grabbed him, went to the counter, and said, "Ring him up. This one's mine." Then I put him in my purse. I took him home that night, proudly held him up aloft to Ronnie, and announced, "Look what I'm giving Mr. Hall for Christmas!"

Ronnie stared at me blankly, then said, "You don't give Manly Hall a teddy bear for Christmas." Ronnie called in Arthur who was equally dismayed by my alarming choice of gift. They made me feel bad, but I put my Capricorn-double-Taurus foot down. "He gets the bear." When confronted with the situation, Edith's expression seemed to ask if I was devoid of reason. But she held no sway upon my determination. When Christmas arrived and we went over to the Halls for dinner, I brought the bear with me.

When I presented the bear to Mr. Hall he cried, "Toby!" He told me that he had a bear just like that when he was a child. He held it like he'd found his long-lost friend. I wish I had a picture of the look on my face when I turned and smiled at Ronnie. He was already smiling at me. That time *I* got to do the Groucho eyebrows.

TWO FUNERALS

One morning at PRS Ronnie walked up to me with a perturbed expression. He told me Mr. Hall wasn't feeling well. He asked Ronnie to substitute for him. Not a lecture, a funeral. I was none too pleased. I did not want that morbid boy giving a speech surrounded by the grief stricken in a garden of cadavers. And I was certainly not going along as driver. Arthur Johnson volunteered for that honor.

At the event, the puzzled funeral staff gathered themselves up to deal with this unusually young and non-denominational eulogizer. They joined the other skeptics graveside. The guest of honor at the funeral happened to be the wife of a poet. There her husband sat, without her for the first time in decades. Their love was a romantic legend in their family and at PRS. Standing by the casket, a feeling of emptiness overcame the boy. He described how a flock of birds took flight from the cemetery unseen by those gathered. They were impatient to be done with a past that they were ready to surrender.

Ronnie told me the widower's stare haunted him. The old poet stared at him disapprovingly. Why would a young man in love waste precious time standing by a stranger's grave? Delivering a spiritually uplifting eulogy to an audience half evangelical Christian and half Vedic was no easy task, but Ronnie performed so well he was asked back for a second funeral not long after, since husband soon followed wife to be reunited in the great beyond.

❖

Ronnie became more attentive to me. He wanted to know how I really felt about any and every thing. He often surprised me with gifts. He was still a domineering guy, as he had been raised to be, but the glimmer of light I had seen from the start grew brighter. Ronnie thought Mr. Hall had sent him to the funerals deliberately. But that's how it is when you're in harmony with the Dao; you can't tell the difference between the coincidental and the intentional.

A WEDDING

Okay, the marriage thing. Please understand, Ronnie and I had both come from families where marriage meant people staying together to hate each other for the rest of their lives. We were best friends, we were in love, we were happy; why would we want to ruin that with marriage? Words like *wife* and *husband* made us cringe.

Ronnie had already proposed. In Tasmania, in a wild animal reserve with pink ibises tapping the table around us, their long beaks seeking treats. I accepted. But we both knew that it was just between the two of us.

Meanwhile, Arthur Johnson had discovered a treasure trove of recordings of early lectures by MPH that were being made available for the first time in cassette sets. Pat Ervin was mighty happy with Arthur about that. He helped bring some major revenue in and made Mr. Hall's students very grateful.

PRS celebrated fifty years of incorporation. Mr. Hall turned eighty-three, but he could still deliver a flawless ninety-minute lecture. Since spending time there meant more time with Ronnie, I would drive over after work.

Okay, I'll stop avoiding the subject. One day Ronnie got called into the office because Mr. Hall wanted to talk to him about something important. He was to bring "Tanya." When we got there he and Marie were conferring over our astrological charts. She was flipping her keys around, having arrived to drive him home. Mr. Hall explained that they'd like to talk with us about our charts over dinner. I didn't know what to expect. Being the perpetual optimist, I figured something was wrong.

Dinner was pleasant enough. No ugly astrological revelations. But they were clearly acting suspiciously as far as I was concerned. Then the announcement came. After careful analysis the Halls had decided that we should get married. Ronnie protested. With his parents a wedding was out of the question. So Mr. Hall doubled down. He and Marie would choose the day for the wedding; in fact, they had already picked out three potential dates. Marie added that she would make sure the sun was in the tenth house so we could carry on her work.

To my relief Ronnie was having none of it. So Mr. Hall anted up again. He would marry us himself in their backyard under the double tree. Ronnie faltered. But he demanded time for us to consider and discuss this diabolical turn of events.

I was scared in a new way. A deep down in your soul scare. I felt my relationship was in jeopardy. They were threatening our good thing. This could fuck everything up. Even if the Halls had looked at our charts, and even though I could see in their own marriage what seemed like a lasting love, I was counting on Ronnie's parents to throw the usual blocks. To my shock they didn't.

My mom was happy I wouldn't be living in sin anymore. But I didn't see much of her anyway, and hadn't for quite some time. She had moved up north and her Church of Christ thing gave her a warped perspective. But I'll give her this: at least she was okay with me getting married by a hoodoo guy like Mr. Hall. She didn't care as long as it was legal.

So now what? What do we have to do to get this thing over with? I wondered in my romantic Capricorn way. We got the marriage license. PRS babied us along at each step. I made sure no one from my family would be there. No hostile brother to show me up on my wedding day, like at my graduation, my birthdays, and any other event that was important to me.

I drove myself to my own wedding. I needed to feel I had some control. Richard, Edith, and members of Ronnie's family met me out front. They were quite nervous. They told me I was late and asked, How could any woman possibly be late to her own wedding? But behind the front door Marie was lying in wait, plotting further delays. She wanted that wedding chart sun in the tenth house.

Mr. Hall wanted the sun in the eleventh house, more sociable and friendly. But Marie's mission, which Ronnie and I were now apparently designated to fulfill, required sun in the tenth house for maximum visibility of her work. Mr. Hall had pointed out several times that with our strong Saturn placements Ronnie and I preferred privacy. Marie would end the discussion with an intolerant, "Nonsense!"

Mr. Hall, looking serious in his black robes and a big Hermetic cross, went outside to stand in the sun as if to say, Let's get this show on the road. The guests gathered as, with his Holy Bible in hand, he assumed the position under the double tree in front of the teahouse that seemed now more like a shrine.

But Marie grabbed my arm and physically held me back. Mr. Hall stood outside squinting in our direction. Lynn Blessing and Edith told Marie to let me go. She peered at a clock on the other side of the room. Eventually, Marie released the bride, but only after she had gotten her sun in the tenth house.

So there I stood under the double tree with my bouquet of irises in honor of the goddess of rainbows. I must have looked nervous because Mr. Hall, Ronnie, George, and Victor assured me everything would be okay.

Mr. Hall began the ceremony, so Ronnie and I looked at each other. Ronnie smiled at me. Love took over. I was impressed when Mr. Hall artfully mumbled something that could have been mistaken for my name. I appreciated the effort. When Mr. Hall mentioned being a priest of the Order of Melchizedek, it seemed to me we were getting married in all dimensions, not just one. Right after he pronounced us man and wife we kissed. My friend's baby let out with a gleeful squeal that made everyone laugh. Arthur Johnson recorded the wedding ceremony. We got a cassette. I found it recently, stuck in a shoebox with a bunch of demos and rehearsal recordings from our band.

The Halls, Edith, even Pat, joined us at Siamese Princess. We all drank champagne that afternoon. For our wedding present, the Halls gave us a Japanese midnight scroll of gold and indigo ink representing Amitaba, the Buddha of Infinite Light and of the paradise known as the Western Pure Land, and his assistants Mahāsthāmaprāpta, whose name means strength arrives, on the left and, on the right, Avalokiteshvara, bodhisattva of compassion. That spring Pearl in her "Happenings at Headquarters" section of *PRS Journal* announced Ronnie's marriage to "Tamara." At least it wasn't Tanya. She and Ronnie are described as "close personal friends of Mr. and Mrs. Hall."

The Christmas after our wedding the Halls gave us another beautiful Japanese Buddhist scroll, a folk version of the Buddhist Wheel of Karma in earthy deep colors. They also gave us a gift of three beautiful prints of Chinese musicians. Mr. Hall explained that they were test prints made during the restoration of a temple. At the time I didn't consider it a suggestion for a vocation. But it's a hell of a coincidence that I wound up touring in a three-piece band.

THE SOCIETY
OF FIVE FELLOWS

A topic of conversation among the regulars when I was at PRS was the uncanny way that dubious Christians touring the library would inevitably open the copy of the big book on display to the page where a sorcerer is raising an elemental, or some other Satanic-looking illustration. That book is like a mirror reflecting the beholder. The library itself had a serendipitous quality. People told stories of the right book falling into their hands. But it could unexpectedly shock you with something inconceivable.

There it was under a box in the bottom shelf. The most irresistible looking issue of Mr. Hall's journal *Horizon*. Sharp gold lettering on a black cover. "The Magazine of Useful and Intelligent Living." Dated August 1941. Paris had fallen the summer before. The Nazis were driving deep into Russia. London had been set afire by bombs. The Blitz had been raging for almost a year. The Japanese attack on Pearl Harbor was only three months away. Intrigued by this glam issue of *Horizon,* Ronnie retrieved it from the drawer.

He found me in the gift shop. We sat outside on a bench. Roses scented the air. You could hear the traffic on Los Feliz Boulevard, but it seemed so much more distant than it actually was. He opened the booklet. We were surprised to find it was marbled blue on the inside.

As he turned the pages we smiled, until we saw the title "The Jew Does Not Fit In."

This excerpt from a lecture on the Kabbala was clearly meant to draw the attention of anti-Semites and convert them to a more civilized view. It's a strange experience reading the words "If we were to exterminate any race because of unpleasant members there would not be a race left on earth" when you're sitting next to a Jewish kid. Mr. Hall wrote that right about the time that most of Ronnie's family were being rounded up for extermination.

"Should we ask him about it?" I offered. Ronnie said the piece was spectacularly tone deaf. Using a phrase like "one life, one race, one purpose, one destiny," even if what Mr. Hall meant is that we're all brothers and sisters in the human race, rang more Hitler than Gandhi. We sat in silence for a moment. "What is there to ask him?" Ronnie finally said. "He's working with me. He knows my parents are Holocaust survivors. He's seen the numbers on my father's arm." So we never brought it up. We simply tucked the issue back where Ronnie had found it. A secret left for someone else to discover and probably misinterpret.

One of the best kept secrets at PRS was the existence of the Society of Five Fellows. I don't know who came up with the idea: Ronnie, Arthur, Lynn Blessing, Dave, or Walt, a thirty-third degree Mason whose day gig was painting portraits of horses. Walt was quiet and obviously a sweet guy, a real family man. As the only non-musician in the group he made sure to contribute something of value at every meeting. They always seemed to meet on rainy nights, in the PRS library with Mr. Hall's blessing. I know they lit candles because I bought them. I was mainly relieved that as a non-fellow I would not be expected to attend.

At worst, I feared this might be another outbreak of initiate fever. What's worse than one fellow with initiate fever? Five. Or it could be some maneuver to recruit Ronnie for whatever nefarious scheme, well intentioned or not, they might be harboring. Ronnie assured me he wouldn't lend anyone any money. But these musicians were pretty down to earth. They were more inclined to sarcastic quips than ambitious plans. They hatched ideas for a few cool events that happened later at PRS, including Arthur's lute recitals. They shared insights gathered from their most recent studies.

I imagine each of them looked into the shadowy depths of the library, dimly lit by candlelight. I knew from personal experience the gravity of that library at night, with all those books and religious objects. It's difficult to describe this in a reasonable way. A place dense with thought and intent. As if the ghostly authors and the former owners of every book enshrined there had gathered in the silence.

As always Ronnie reported the fellowship's activities to me like we were on an anthropological expedition. They weren't doing seances. There was no Ouija board. No one conjured. They did not perform rituals. There were no schemes. No ceremonies. No outfits. Though each had a miniature version of Mr. Hall's Hermetic Cross, a gift from a Mason.

They had access to the typed notes from lectures Mr. Hall had given early in his career, when he was more inclined to talk about occult matters. They discussed Proclus the Neoplatonist, Paracelsus the alchemist, and Eliphas Levi. Dave had a collection of Thomas Taylor first editions that even Mr. Hall could have envied. In the late eighteenth and early nineteenth centuries, Taylor published what are now considered dreadful translations of works by Plato, Aristotle, Plotinus, Porphyry, and Proclus. However difficult his translations, Taylor had a deep understanding of his subject. His contemporaries ridiculed him as a pagan, joking that he would sacrifice a bull on the day of Zeus. But Mary Wollstonecraft, author of *A Vindication of the Rights of Woman* in 1792, whose life was a constant battle, said the only peace she had ever known was in the library of Thomas Taylor, her landlord. There she read and napped, while Taylor wrote.

Taylor's translations are clumsy and sometimes downright wrong. But he made philosophical treasures of antiquity available for the first time in English. His translations influenced William Blake,

Percy Shelley, William Wordsworth, Ralph Waldo Emerson, Bronson Alcott, and even Allen Ginsberg. Taylor also wrote a book that argued for the rights of animals; he was a vegetarian.

As for the Five Fellows, it's doubtful that they aspired to eventually become something like the Order of the Golden Dawn. All but one were musicians and so not inclined to commit to any group that would have them, even a group they started themselves. The meetings became less frequent until by the end of the year no one brought them up anymore. They had other things they had to do. But who am I to talk? At that time I still had no idea I was a musician. Arthur was right, I was completely out of my mind; but so was Thomas Taylor.

THE ICE CRACKS

Pearl's husband Charlie used to hang out in the PRS library while she worked. He was an amiable but senile elder, somehow boyish in old age. He liked to talk to Ronnie. Mostly he talked about how clearly he could still remember running through the tall green grass of his boyhood. He could still feel it brushing his legs as he ran. He smiled ear to ear as he remembered childhood. But then he'd turn wistful, as he looked into space while marveling at the passage of time. No wonder a moment later he'd be confused. Then he was gone. Passed away in the night. Pearl showed up for work as usual. She seemed more relieved than grief-stricken, but perhaps that was a facade. Or maybe she had grieved his loss long ago.

In the PRS Bookstore, Ronnie's "Let's Create a Renaissance" lecture on cassette (inspired by Ficino, the original Renaissance man) was displayed in the glass case right next to Mr. Hall's latest, and it stayed there, a steady bestseller. Ronnie understood if he wanted it he could have made a career out of this situation. But he was not a happy camper. He foresaw a lonely life as a metaphysical writer and lecturer with a neglected wife.

To keep the large audience he attracted, Ronnie felt he had to constantly censor himself so as not to alienate anyone. He had to fulfill their expectations rather than his own. People wanted him to focus on self-help. Like Mr. Hall, Ronnie's favorite source of inspiring stories was history. But even Mr. Hall had found himself retreating from in-depth looks at complex subjects like Neoplatonism in favor of simply helping people cope. That's no less noble a mission, but Ronnie wasn't feeling it. I was glad he understood that, being a mess himself, he might not be the best life coach.

At PRS cracks were showing in the ice. Mr. Hall's dream had been to publish a companion volume to *The Secret Teachings of All Ages,* but this one would be focused on the history of Asian mysticism, mysteries, magic, and religions. He put Ronnie to work gathering materials. Every day Mr. Hall would add an illustration, a paragraph, a page to the ever-growing file. Every night Ronnie brought the file home. He tried to help by researching the most modern studies on the subject, but he found that a wave of new scholarship meant that Mr. Hall wouldn't have time to study all the new books. By definition his latest magnum opus could not be the best possible resource for students that Mr. Hall intended it to be.

While working on that book, Mr. Hall told Ronnie about the *Kongokai* and *Taizokai* mandalas of the Japanese *Shingon* tradition of esoteric Buddhism. Meditating on these mandalas the practitioners would imprint every detail in their minds, eventually visualizing combining the mandalas, envisioning how they connected at every point.

The Kongokai mandala represents the pure world of the Diamond Realm, the Great Realization, the unchanging cosmic principle. The Taizokai mandala represents the Womb Realm, the Matrix World, the active physical realm of compassion. I was charmed by the description of the ritual when a blindfolded Shingon novice throws a flower on the mandala. Where the flower lands determines which Buddha they will devote themselves to as they begin meditation and memorization. Mr. Hall was one of the first writers in English to examine these mandalas and practices in detail.

The big file I got to peruse nightly eventually became one of Mr. Hall's last books: *Meditation Symbols in Eastern and Western Mysticism: Mysteries of the Mandala,* published after we'd left. Of all the books that contributed to that book, the only one that stayed in the small shelf behind Mr. Hall's desk, the one that Ronnie simply had to have a copy of, was Pierre Rambach's *The Secret Message of Tantric Buddhism,* a beautiful art book published by Rizzoli. There are no dirty pictures in it, so don't get your hopes up.

Meanwhile, college had unforeseen ramifications. Ronnie's faculty advisor was Yale doctorate Kenneth Atchity, a worldwide expert on Homer and Dante, known around Occidental College as the Dragon Lord. He did not find Mr. Hall academically sound. He gave Ronnie hotly intolerant stares when subjects came up like Bacon writing the Shakespeare plays. He advised Ronnie to read Borges. Not that he was recruiting Ronnie for academia. He wasn't the only professor to tell Ronnie to avoid an academic career, but he was the only one who actually left academia. He became a movie producer.

Ronnie graduated Phi Beta Kappa after getting his degree in two and a half years. His GRE score gave me a nose bleed. Now we had to choose between graduate school and the opportunities for expanding his career that others began offering. A lecture circuit, a book contract, he could be a metaphysical teacher on his own, without PRS, we were told.

But Ronnie saw what I was seeing. People who wanted to be of service to humanity but who were spinning themselves into knots. From what I could tell, what they really wanted was attention. What they would do with it depended on the person. Some wanted money. Some were in it for sex. Some wanted fame, which they thought would bring them the other two. But most of them wanted to have authority. To be considered experts. Most of all they wanted to be believed. But many of these people trying to live spiritual missions were living unexamined lives. The temple of initiates suddenly looked like a shed full of hungry ghosts.

When I needed to be alone at PRS I found refuge in the neglected back parking lot. Most people didn't even know it was there. It had its own driveway. Were they pepper or eucalyptus trees that gave the place its quiet separateness? I'd sit on the wall, kicking my feet, thinking over everything. Where we had come from. All the possibilities moving forward. In the afternoon, the breeze from the Pacific made it all the way to Los Feliz, rustling the trees. The patience needed to allow the world to unfold in front of you is not easy to achieve.

Around this time I started drawing cartoons in a notebook during Ronnie's lectures, cataloging behaviors I observed among his flock. For instance, "The Enlightened Teacher." You could find these guys any day of the week at Bodhi Tree Bookstore, twice as many on the weekend. A crude drawing of a guy in robes with his arms raised and his gaze aloft as if receiving direct confirmation from the Divine. Sure of his personal importance, he smiles ear to ear. In the next panel he's at the wheel of his car impatiently honking at a senior with a cane in the crosswalk.

Another cartoon. A wide-eyed novice proclaiming his purity and the elimination of the negative. Behind him a big shadow with horns rises and grins a mouthful of spiky teeth, saying, "Oh, yoo-hoo!"

REGULARS

Over dinner one night, Mr. Hall told us a joke. At an emergency meeting of a chapter of the Theosophical Society the members awaited an important announcement. A lady stood up proclaiming, after great study and much reflection, that she was the reincarnation of Hypatia the Neoplatonist philosopher, mathematician, and astronomer of ancient Alexandria. The Hidden Masters had confirmed this. Another leapt to her feet. "That is impossible," she shouted, "I was Hypatia!" Soon every woman at the table was shouting, "I was Hypatia!"

Among Mr. Hall's followers were people who believed he was St. Germain or the reincarnation of Blavatsky; he would save the world from World War III or no earthquake could happen in Los Angeles as long as he was around. Some believed Mr. Hall could read minds. Some of the letters Ronnie read for Mr. Hall involved weird dreams that the dreamers thought must be of extreme significance. They thought Mr. Hall had actually visited them and so they were getting in touch to let him know they got the message and were awaiting further instructions.

Mr. Hall liked to call himself a rogue scholar. But to these people he was a savior who could rescue them from rotten marriages, bad jobs, and despondent lives. He tried to tell them that they must save themselves. He wanted to inspire people to keep looking for the answers within, not without. Expert at rekindling optimism, he warmed many a discouraged heart.

I met many intelligent, elegant human beings who populated Mr. Hall's flock. The regulars were people who had cultivated a lifetime of philosophy, culture, art, and antiquarian book collecting.

Irene Bird, as her name implies, looked like someone who would have fit right in with that table of old-time theosophists in Mr. Hall's Hypatia joke. A realtor from Los Alamitos, California, Irene had been attending lectures at PRS since 1964. For a time she and her husband Dr. Byron Bird led the PRS Headquarters Discussion Group. A big woman who wore brightly-colored dresses that flowed like sails, she reminded me of a galleon on the open sea. With her long red hair piled atop her head, you could easily picture her as a nineteenth-century suffragette. We often heard her voice, or joyous laughter, ringing out over the crowd after Mr. Hall's Sunday lectures. She became a regular at Ronnie's lectures as well. She once told us she first met Mr. Hall in a dream.

Judson and Nadine Harris were an urbane older couple. Obviously deeply in love, they seemed to be involved in a never-ending conversation with each other, with a love of learning that was carrying them nicely through their eighties. Old-school elegant, they mailed us thank-you notes with helpful suggestions after Ronnie's lectures. They had been attending Mr. Hall's Sunday mornings for over thirty years.

Another regular was Dr. William Abt, who introduced himself one evening. A blind man of about ninety, he nevertheless navigated Greater Los Angeles by public transportation using only an intricately carved and colorfully painted cane. He offered to take us out to lunch. One afternoon he came to our apartment for a visit. He was trying to teach us something about aging. He told us to start a good program like yoga and keep it going all our lives. He told us not to let our minds get in the way of our physical abilities. To demonstrate, this man effortlessly popped into a headstand. I still can't do a headstand. But thanks to him I learned yoga.

More advice from Dr. Abt. Use your hand like a cup and rinse out your mouth when you can't brush after a meal. Teeth are the foundation of health, he kept reminding us. This simple practice he claimed would prevent most cavities. A retired osteopath, Abt had treated many injured hands caused by people spreading out their fingers to push off the ground when standing up. Losing balance, he pointed out, you can easily break or dislocate a finger, and people do. So make a fist when you support your body weight with your hands, like a good simian. We were later told that Dr. Abt was not a PRS regular, or at least nobody remembered seeing him at anyone else's lectures, not even Sundays with Mr. Hall.

AMONG
THE HUNGRY GHOSTS

Since Ronnie was answering Mr. Hall's correspondence and proved himself to be trustworthy, Mr. Hall gave him more responsibility. Ronnie would now screen in person the people who wanted to meet Mr. Hall. Ronnie met some colorful characters, many of them sweet and well intentioned. Some were a little too enthusiastic about things that didn't really add up. One fellow swore he could photograph auras, but Mr. Hall would have to be nude for the session. A father tormented his family with plans to save the world. A conspiracy theorist had the key that unlocks it all. A steady stream of reincarnated spiritual celebrities. And the many urgent messages that couldn't be divulged to anyone but the man himself, so there must be a meeting in person.

Ronnie also saw the darker side of what Mr. Hall had to deal with. People who believed they were possessed by spirits because their roommates performed a magical ritual. Or the guy who thought he was really growing a third eye right out of his forehead. People with houses haunted by hostile ghosts. People who couldn't turn off their psychic sensitivities. And so many of them. You really would need all the hands of Avalokiteshvara to deal with the multitude of requests for help.

Mr. Hall was a wise old man with some answers in a world full of sad seekers of mercy. Compassion comes at a high cost if you're only human. Trying to bestow a kindness, Mr. Hall would give Ronnie a message for each, and then Ronnie would have to turn them away. Some believed a meeting with Manly Hall to be their last hope.

Pleased by Ronnie's progress, Mr. Hall explained that when metaphysical teachers asked to meet him, most just wanted a photo to enhance their mystique and lend credibility to their reputations. Ronnie would now screen them. "Be sure to take her with you," Mr. Hall looked at me. "I want you to tell me what you see." So began my short and tragic career as Mr. Hall's screener.

When we returned from our first mission Ronnie gave the "all clear." Mr. Hall turned to me. I shook my head no, "I wouldn't let that guy feed my cat." Mr. Hall chuckled. I always noticed some telling detail. Soon I was screener number one. Mr. Hall taught me the great art of listening and saying nothing.

As Ronnie would handle conversations with people we screened, and they would dismiss me as the pretty girlfriend, I could settle back and watch them perform. My wait for the reveal was seldom disappointed. Somewhere usually between two-thirds and three-quarters of their way through, when they thought they were really selling it, they'd look over at me and notice that I'd been watching them with a cold eye.

I was rooting for everyone who wanted to meet Mr. Hall. Look what meeting him did for me. But no hustler or lowlife was going to get by me, and how you treat the least is a good test; I was always assumed to be the least. I was accustomed to that.

And so I met many casualties of spirituality gone wrong. The seekers of wisdom who were actually seeking dominion. The ceremonial magicians who opened portals they could not close into realms they could not understand. The positive thinkers whose shadows erupted into inexplicably negative predicaments. The prosperity teachers who never really succeeded at anything. The humble Christians obsessed with self-aggrandizing missions. The white men convinced they were gurus of Eastern lineages. The paranormal researchers who discovered entities that would not leave them alone. The psychics who could not shut down their reception of the thoughts and feelings of others. The hucksters repackaging metaphysical teachings as personality cults. What a world of cliques, competition, and manipulation was revealed!

THE YELLOW SWEATER
CULT

A famous metaphysical author, teacher, and astrologer from eastern Europe, with a worldwide following, was going to be in Los Angeles and wished to confer with Manly Hall, a fellow enlightened master. Mr. Hall was skeptical. He wanted us to screen the guy before it went any further.

We drove down Sunset Boulevard late one morning, from the rainbow flags of West Hollywood straight through Beverly Hills and its mansions with acres of ludicrously long lonely lawns. Winding past the pink oleanders and coast redwoods of UCLA, we drove over the metal-and-glass river that is the 405 freeway and down toward the beach. Before we could see the glare of the Pacific we took a small side street that led to a dirt road in the foothills. All around us dry weeds glowed California sunlight.

As we approached the parking area, we encountered a fellow in a pale-yellow sweater, anxiously normal, the kind of normal that makes normal people nervous. As we drove to our space we saw another guy that looked like the first one, down to the pale yellow sweater and his haircut. Then a female of the same species, nearly indistinguishable from the males. Then a flock.

As we walked through the dirt parking lot I was surprised by the number of luxury cars. Luxury cars were few and far between at PRS.

The devotees scrutinized our friend, the photographer Renee Ravel, the only person to go with us from the world of music to the world of metaphysics. Renee wore Cleopatra eye makeup and matching jewelry. A henna-haired Capricorn, she fancied all things ancient Egyptian, so much so she drove a gold VW Beetle with the license plate Kephra (the golden scarab that pushes the sun across the sky).

If she wasn't reprehensible looking enough, Ronnie had begun to grow his hair out and I was dressed all in black on a sunny Sunday morning. Clearly we were three primary examples of what should not be allowed. To the chagrin of the greeter at the entrance to the large Quonset hut, we were revealed to be none other than the emissaries of Manly Palmer Hall. Suspicion evaporated into obsequious kindness. Well, not entirely. The woman in charge began to lead us to the front row. Ronnie insisted we stay near the back due to time constraints. It would be rude to leave from the front row. We took seats near the door. She didn't like that.

Unlike PRS where people were friendly and sociable, this crowd was very serious, and the vibe was "you should be too." Strangely enough, the man of the hour had a much younger and very attractive woman up front where he was going to be delivering his talk. She had the composed authority of a first lady, but I never found out who she was.

The master in question took the stage. We later dubbed him Swami Moses. He had a well-cultivated white beard, long white hair, dressed in white, and a very white audience. He squinted at the crowd during an extremely long and uncomfortable silence, until a handsome little blue jay came hopping into the doorway to stand squawking. No one laughed. The audience members nodded to each other and gazed adoringly at their guru, knowing his purity must have attracted this innocent creature.

Now here is a venture into Tamra's mind. That bird was trained. He showed up to get his treat. When he didn't get it promptly, he squawked once and flew away.

After basking for a few moments in the adoration, Swami Moses began lecturing in French, while a translator reverently delivered his wisdom. First thing I noticed was the way he used repetition in his speech and the lulling cadence of hypnosis. He rolled his *r's* like they were Havana cigars. Unlike Mr. Hall's lectures that emphasized self-determination and finding the teacher within, Swami Moses complained about promiscuity more than a mother of teenagers. He mentioned repeatedly that no one else had recognized the astrological revelations he shared. I had the feeling what was happening in that Quonset hut was not so much shared wisdom as personality cult. He was comfortable being called master. This was the kind of thing that Mr. Hall was always pushing away. Now I'm not saying that the man had no truth to tell nor good to give; maybe he was just being taken advantage of, or maybe I had it all wrong. But I knew he was not going to meet Mr. Hall.

As if he read my mind (or was I reading his) Ronnie turned to me and said: "Let's go." We rose. The woman who disapproved of our choice of seating now saw her worst expectations realized. She blocked our exit. She narrowed her eyes at us, demanding to know where we were going. Ronnie at first attempted to be merely polite, explaining he had seen what he needed and had to be getting back, it was a long drive. She stood in our way frowning. Ronnie tried to speak in a way she could understand: "My master is calling me. I must go." That gave her pause, but she still stood in our way so Ronnie raised the stakes: "We'll try to make it back here," he lied. She stepped aside, arms folded in contempt, and said: "I hope so, for your sakes." I remember how grateful I felt as we drove away, as if I had escaped.

Ronnie reported back to Mr. Hall the large and prosperous crowd attracted by Swami Moses. He thought if they enjoyed the Swami's tepid lecture, they would love Sundays at PRS and a more relaxed atmosphere. Mr. Hall chuckled. Ronnie continued. So maybe it might be worthwhile to have a photo with Swami Moses so that some of his followers might consider PRS as a destination? After all, astrology, Kabbala, and other shared interests made for a natural crossover.

I was shaking my head no. Mr. Hall held up his hand and stopped

Ronnie. "What did you see?" he asked me. "That's a bad man," I said. "Why?" Mr. Hall asked. "His effect on his followers made them act like robots. That kind of conformity scares me." I told him about the blue bird and he rolled his eyes as if to say, "Oh, the old scrub jay routine." I thought that was the end of it, but it was really the beginning of the end of everything.

ONE VERY BAD APPLE

We were told someone from the community of Swami Moses wanted to jump ship to PRS. The Halls had met him at a fundraiser. They thought he seemed like a decent fellow. We were asked to screen him. His name was Daniel Fritz, and he claimed to be a reincarnated Atlantean priest.

The Halls had told us that Atlantis was a place where science lost all ethics, where scientists tinkered together human animal hybrids, like they're supposedly working on in China as I write this. They said the people of Atlantis enslaved the world to feed their need for the best of everything. They were greedy, hungry for power, and without conscience or compassion. Time would reveal that Fritz had these characteristics of the past life he claimed. He was either a criminal or a tragic clown or both.

I was skeptical of Fritz given where he'd come from, but I remembered to remain open-minded, to greet him with emptiness as always. We met him in the PRS library. The library was closed on an overcast day. With the lights off the dimly-lit room seemed to doze.

One bright light glowed down from the catwalk above, illuminating Fritz sitting center stage at the long rectangular table. He had a notebook. He was reading *Transcendental Magic, Its Doctrine and Ritual* by Eliphas Levi, with two books by Mr. Hall at the ready. He was the picture of the perfect student.

Ronnie and I walked over. We introduced ourselves. We were

cordial as we sat across from him at the table. Ronnie conveyed greetings from Mr. Hall. Fritz told us how grateful he felt to be at PRS. He marveled at the library and the service Mr. Hall had done. He offered to help Mr. Hall however he could. He mentioned how much he'd like to work for him.

Ronnie asked questions about what Fritz was studying and what he would like to talk to Mr. Hall about. Fritz was evasive, his vague answers presented with a neophyte's enthusiasm. This wasn't a meeting, it was an audition. He was saying exactly what he was supposed to say, but he had the malicious look of a determined rat trying to get into the granary.

Ronnie and Fritz bantered, a fencing match of banalities; neither revealed anything to the other. When we got up to leave I offered to shake Fritz's hand. I wanted to be gracious since I was representing Mr. Hall and PRS. I felt like I shook the cold clammy hand of a Ring Wraith. He had the irritated expression of someone who has touched something unclean. He wanted to dismiss me, but he didn't like what he saw in my eyes, my certainty that I was looking at a hustler.

Ronnie turned to me after we walked out the doors of the library, "I don't like that guy," he said. "He made my skin crawl," I responded. Ronnie looked very serious. We were both disturbed, though Fritz had said nothing disturbing. We stood there for a couple minutes in the courtyard as clouds passed unnoticed above us.

I felt like Fritz made the room colder and darker. It's hard to describe that profoundly disturbing feeling, like meeting a predator on the way to its prey. We reported our impressions of Fritz to Mr. Hall and I was severe in my warning that I had a bad feeling about him. MPH gravely nodded his head.

A few weeks later, to my surprise, I saw Fritz sitting alone in the library again. I turned to Ronnie, "What's he doing here?" We asked Edith what was going on. She said the Halls had become friendly with Fritz. On our next visit to their home Ronnie asked Marie about that. Marie's excitement about Fritz was obvious. He got her work. He would use computers to help spread her message of salvation to the entire world. He was going to get her a computer of her own.

Back at PRS, Ronnie and I asked for a meeting with Mr. Hall. For the second time I warned him about Fritz. Mr. Hall listened politely. He asked if we had any further information to share, any evidence. We didn't. But then, to our relief, we heard that Fritz had left for Hawaii to start a birthing center where gullible couples could give birth to future spiritual masters in a lagoon of happy dolphins.

What we didn't know was that the Halls had loaned him money for his venture and that they had thrown a send-off party for him at their house. Apparently, Fritz brought a bevy of pregnant ladies with him, no doubt gaining credibility from the endorsement of the Halls. But we didn't know about any of that yet. We thought the danger had passed.

THE CURTAIN FALLS

Mr. Hall asked Ronnie to see him at home, not PRS. "Ron," Mr. Hall said, "I want you to go." Naturally, Ronnie asked why. Mr. Hall explained that all those wonderful elders, including himself, who had shown us such kindness weren't long for this world. He did not want us to witness the demise of PRS. "This is my flock," he told Ronnie, "and I have to take them home."

Ronnie took this as a test of his loyalty. So he refused to leave. But Mr. Hall kept telling him to leave. So Ronnie began proposing potential futures. Mr. Hall was not willing to tell him what to do, other than study Chinese, but he was willing to comment on Ronnie's choices.

Ronnie wondered if he should get an Ivy League Ph.D. then return to help legitimize PRS? After all, Duke University offered him a house to live in and a salary. Ronnie got into Harvard Divinity. Mr. Hall shook his head no.

"But what about PRS?" Ronnie asked. Mr. Hall looked straight into his eyes as he made clear that he did not care what happened to PRS once he was gone. It had served his purpose well, and while he would leave guidelines for its future as he saw it, it would be just as well if it turned out to be something else. A degree in psychology? No. Novelist? No. Computer programming? No.

They dragged this out for months. Clearly they still wanted to be friends. It's not that we couldn't take a hint. We really didn't want to leave, and we didn't know where to go. I would sit cross-legged on the floor in our apartment as Ronnie's latest report left me wondering if our time at PRS had been an ephemeral sanctuary. Were we headed back to what we had known before? Mr. Hall assured Ronnie that with his intelligence and his good heart whatever he did would turn out well. Ronnie wasn't accepting generalities or the brush-off. He wanted the approval of his mentor for whatever his next dedication in life would be.

One overcast day, when Mr. Hall's office felt gloomy, I was there when Ronnie offered up a choice he felt certain Mr. Hall would reject. "Well, I came here from music; maybe I should go back?" Now perhaps Mr. Hall had simply tired of the questions and had made up his mind to say yes to whatever Ronnie came up with next. But to our shock Mr. Hall folded his hands on his chest, closed his eyes, and nodded in agreement. No more inspections of the Japanese altar or lunches in the vault.

Oh, lucky me. As the old saying I just invented goes, "The only thing worse than a musician's girlfriend is a musician's wife." Now my fate was sealed, because unbeknownst to me this was the path that would lead directly to me becoming a musician.

While the maestro and the boy continued their long goodbye, nothing changed for Ronnie and me at PRS. We didn't tell anyone what he said to us or that we would be leaving. At this point I believe Ronnie thought if he quietly continued performing his work, Mr. Hall would allow him to stay on indefinitely. Ronnie was still a popular lecturer at PRS. Mr. Hall kept giving us tasks. We were still his screeners, but not for long.

CASSANDRA

Then I saw Fritz in the PRS library again. He was talking to Edith. They seemed friendly. I couldn't believe my eyes. My stomach sank. What ill storm had washed him back up on our shore? Edith explained that Fritz had insinuated himself into the Hall's household as Mr. Hall's daily caregiver. She seemed pleased because Mr. Hall was exercising and losing weight.

Soon after, on a bright afternoon, quite unannounced, the only time we ever used that privilege, we visited the Halls. Call it a surprise welfare check. Fritz answered the door and was obviously unhappy to see us. He told us we could not see the Halls without an appointment. Ronnie informed him that the Halls had told us we could drop in any time. Marie recognized Ronnie's voice. She told Fritz to show us in. For an instant he scowled, then he smiled as he swung open the door.

As we socialized with the Halls he scurried here, then there, pretending to be busy, pausing to eavesdrop in adjacent rooms, hovering around doorways, wherever he landed casting a mantis shadow. But the Halls seemed to be themselves. Marie was more animated than ever, as she explained that Fritz not only made them organic food, he also had bought her a computer and found helpers to teach her how to use it. She felt confident that computers had been invented to help her spread the good news about the Space Mother. Mr. Hall's face seemed to have a healthy glow. He was humorous, but a little sheepish. I thought he might be concerned that after my warnings about Fritz I might make things uncomfortable, but I kept my opinion to myself. "Maybe we were wrong," Ronnie said as we walked to our car. I glanced back to find Fritz watching us from a window like Norman Bates in *Psycho*.

Soon after, PRS started to buzz with rumors about the questionable and unusual healing practices Fritz used to treat Mr. Hall. Several regulars mentioned that Mr. Hall seemed a bit anxious. Which brings us to the legend in my own mind of the last time I saw Manly Palmer Hall. I guess denials do come in threes. I requested a third meeting about Fritz. In about twenty minutes I went through the seven stages of death, right in front of my boss. Believe it or not, I had maintained a quiet demeanor and manner at PRS that earned me the label patrician. I knew how to maintain my cool. But that day I lost it.

I bargained. I threw Ronnie on the chopping block, promising he would never bother Mr. Hall again. I begged. I got angry. I told him I knew what I was talking about, "I know this guy is up to no good." I could tell from his expression that Mr. Hall had already made up his mind. I blurted out that I felt sure that Fritz would kill him. Mr. Hall put his hand up and said, "That's enough."

A somber gravity magnified the silence in the room as tears ran down my face and I tried to catch my breath. I looked to my left and I saw Edith standing dumbfounded in the doorway to her office. Ronnie gave me that pleading yet threatening glance that men give hysterical women.

My outburst made me suspect. I had gone mad, like Marie, with a crazy conspiracy theory. Then Mr. Hall looked at me with a resignation that made me shrink. I realized he wasn't ignoring the danger. I believe he knowingly embraced Fritz's treachery. Some kind of karmic Buddhist thing? Take the villain down with you?

His last look, thank you, and goodbye conveyed a message I heard clearly: "I told you kids to get out of here. Now be good little Buddhists like I taught you and don't make a scene." He hated firing people, but I knew I was fired. Apologizing to Mr. Hall on our way out, Ronnie didn't realize this was the last time we'd ever see him.

DON'T LOOK BACK

Like two people adrift on a dark sea, all ties with PRS and the Halls were cut after my epic meltdown. I felt gut-wrenching guilt for destroying Ronnie's relationship with them, and mine. If I had only pumped my brakes before I shot my mouth off, would Mr. Hall have listened to me? He had before. But I became hysterical, as the men say. I was too humiliated to go back. Ronnie and I comforted ourselves with the knowledge that finally, as Mr. Hall wished, we had left.

We went to the Huntington Library and Botanical Gardens. I had been going there since I was eight years old on the terrace gazing over a vast lawn at the city in its ugly glory. The Camellia Show was so lovely and peaceful. I always greeted Thomas Lawrence's *Pinkie* and Thomas Gainsborough's *Blue Boy,* hanging opposite each other in the library. The miniature traveling library seemed so exquisite to me I looked forward to seeing it every time. Each tiny book was a classic. I guess you could say the Huntington was my first PRS.

We lingered in the Japanese garden, on the red bridge overlooking the koi pond. Calico-colored fish shimmered as they swam under the bridge. Light glinted on the water and on their scales. We didn't talk much. We knew we were thinking the same things. We felt lost. All that we accomplished had vanished. As a musician, Ronnie was starting from scratch with no equipment, no band mates, and no knowledge of the current scene. Returning to music with all the sensitivities of metaphysics, and without the callouses of dysfunction, turned out to be like visiting a foreign country. An extremely primitive foreign country.

We wandered among the statues of the Huntington, ending up in front of a romantic eighteenth-century French limestone sculpture *Orpheus and Euridice*. I asked Ronnie to tell me their story again. He told me on their wedding day Euridice was murdered. Orpheus was so grief stricken he went into the underworld. His music allowed him to go anywhere. It even charmed Hades so much he struck a deal with Orpheus. He could have her back, as long as he did not turn and look at her until they had both reached the sunlight.

Hades knew the power of his realm. Orpheus became afraid that Hades had tricked him. He believed Eurydice wasn't following him. He resisted the urge to turn. Still, he had become so anxious that when he reached the sunlight he didn't give her long enough to emerge from the dark. To his dismay he looked into her face as she disappeared again, this time without hope of return. Some said that was not Eurydice following Orpheus, but a phantom sent by Zeus to punish Orpheus for breaking the law against the living visiting the dead. The sculpture captured the moment that Orpheus turns, almost holding her in his arms; but as he turns, she is drawn away.

On the freeway, on the long drive home, I knew that unlike Orpheus, I would never look back. But also, in the spirit of "must you tell all, Marie," I confess there was a side of me that had been feeling like if I got another three-hour Space Mother Principle lecture, and the headache that went with it, I'd scream. Did I want to see another desperate seeker after knowledge who had a scam destined for Mr. Hall's money? A lesson in the dark side of fame that I've never forgotten. I was never angry at Mr. Hall for not listening to my warning. I was angry at myself for not getting through to him. I was angry at Fritz. The guy might as well have had "snake oil for sale" written on his forehead, as far as I was concerned. In retrospect, I realize what easy pickings the Halls and PRS were for any grifter who came along. They let the likes of us in there, didn't they?

Of course, even now I miss the genuine sweetness of the Halls. As someone who didn't have loving grandparents, I valued their friendship greatly. I often wondered how they were doing. That they were only a phone call away comforted me. I felt certain they would figure out Fritz was up to no good. I imagined that Pearl, Edith, and Pat could easily handle the situation. Or maybe the wholesomeness would rub off on Fritz, like it did on us.

FALSE SUNRISE

Arthur Johnson called. Fritz had convinced the Halls that good as gold Pat Ervin was scheming to have Mr. Hall committed, then take PRS over. The old man had fired Pat. But a new hero had arrived in the nick of time. Arthur insisted that Ronnie had to come down and meet Mr. Hall's official spokesman, Mike Mitchell, formerly group vice president of planning and control for the Los Angeles Summer Olympics and executive producer of Live Aid.

Mitchell had been one of the organizers of the first Earth Day, but now like Odysseus in Plato's *Republic,* he chose a private life without glory; he intended to preserve the mom-and-pop store integrity of PRS. He would supervise the transition of PRS to the twenty-first century.

By then the old man was spending most of his time at home. Ronnie didn't like seeing someone else using Mr. Hall's office. A lot of beautiful clutter had been cleared. Much of it, we learned later, had been stolen when Fritz was in control and immediately after. Arthur told us when PRS split into factions and loyalty perished, smuggling and theft ensued. Arthur introduced Ronnie as the old man's star pupil. Ronnie explained that Live Aid was one of the things that inspired him to stop lecturing and start a band.

Mitchell responded that he thought Ronnie leaving metaphysics for the music industry was just one more bit of bad karma from that rough event. Next, he shocked Arthur and Ronnie by saying he'd be leaving PRS as soon as possible. Allow me to paraphrase what he told

119

them. As a peacemaker he had to be diplomatic with arms dealers and dictators. But rock band managers and the music biz in general were worse because at least arms dealers and dictators had some semblance of honor. However, neither could compare to the indomitable factions of PRS, the most unreasonable and unbending forces of nature he had ever dealt with.

During the meeting I perched on my favorite spot on the wall in the back parking lot, under the overhanging trees, where a mockingbird sang amid the chatty sparrows. It was getting dark. I hoped no one I knew would see me. I wanted to remain invisible as I reflected on the irony of skulking in the shadows outside a place that had been like a second home to me.

After the meeting Arthur told us he thought Mitchell must be leaving because of Fritz. Fritz had proven a formidable enemy. Whatever anyone told the Halls, they told Fritz. Now no one from PRS was allowed to speak with the Halls except through Fritz. Mitchell wanted to protect Mr. Hall, but the Halls' loyalty to Fritz was absolute. Soon Mr. Hall's office was empty again.

Mitchell went on to further heroic efforts, as an environmentalist, peace activist, and champion in the fight against human and animal trafficking. I wonder if he ever fell asleep while dealing with some horribly stressful situation only to wake up smiling with relief from a nightmare about being back at PRS. I remember thinking, if that's what happened to a man like him, what would have happened to us? Mr. Hall was right; we didn't stand a chance.

TO THE STRONGEST

While an official investigation dragged on, Fritz, Marie, and PRS battled over the valuable copyrights to Mr. Hall's books. The rarest of the books and manuscripts, including many of them I had enjoyed perusing with the maestro and the boy in the vault, became Marie's property. Marie sold them to the Getty Research Institute. She had enormous legal bills to pay. PRS paid over a million in legal fees. But we found out about all that long after the fact. We were in another world by then, out of touch even with Arthur.

On my birthday in 1994, the year that Ronnie and I started Lucid Nation, the band we've been in ever since, the *Los Angeles Times* had a story about bad times at PRS that included an account of Mr. Hall's possible murder. Newspaper in hand, Ronnie walked into our kitchen with a stunned expression. All he had to say was "Mr. Hall." "Is he dead?" Ronnie nodded yes. "Was it Fritz?" I asked flippantly, carrying on with my task of the moment, only to be surprised when Ronnie nodded again. I had to sit down. Ronnie read the rest of the article out loud.

The gruesome details of Mr. Hall's death made me feel hollow. Mr. Hall gave Fritz power-of-attorney over his estate just six days before he died. What were they doing dragging that old man around in an RV on road trips? Between Fritz's extreme medical practices and long hours on the freeway it seemed a simple and effective way to cause natural causes, if you get my meaning. Some are of the opinion that Mr. Hall died of natural causes, but with as little evidence as I have when I say I suspect foul play, as did the judge, LAPD, and the coroner. But no one could prove it.

From the time we left the Halls, until I heard about what happened, I had come to think of my warnings about Fritz as anxiety over leaving PRS. I had transferred my dread to this innocent man. Or maybe I had simply done Mr. Hall's bidding by getting fired. He had repeatedly told us to leave. When I heard the details it was the confirmation of my darkest fears. It wasn't projection, it was premonition. I saw what was going to happen but I couldn't stop it. My job was to protect that man. He heard what I said. My warning didn't matter. As for PRS, it had become the kind of mess that Alexander the Great left when, as he lay dying, his generals asked to whom he would leave his empire and he replied, "to the strongest."

Later I learned that Steven Ross was the last of the regulars to see Mr. Hall. He showed up at the Halls' house unannounced when Fritz happened to be away. They discussed including PRS publications in Steven's new venture. But when Fritz returned he grabbed Steven by the arm and briskly ushered him out the front door. As he closed it Fritz said: "You will never see him again."

Fritz had implemented a clever plan. He convinced the Halls to transfer all their property including their home to their companies. Then he had a living trust drawn up, claiming it would protect them, but naming himself as executor and trustee. Marie had a history of institutionalization and a doctor had found evidence of age-related mental impairment. That left Fritz in control of the house, the bank accounts, the book copyrights, and PRS and everything in it. Although he would not technically own any of it, for all practical purposes when Mr. Hall died Fritz became a multimillionaire. He would allow Marie to continue living in her house, but with no title to it.

Fritz underestimated Marie and PRS. Lawsuits flew as Fritz, Marie, and PRS squared off against each other. Marie fought to see justice done for the husband she believed had been murdered. She even hired a forensic autopsy expert, who exposed the mistakes in the official report.

I knew we had arrived in the last days of a mirage of utopia, already steeply in decline by the time we had left. Hearing now about its collapse into dystopia was like seeing an oasis gone to ruin. Now we understood why Mr. Hall had sent us away. Finding out about his fate lowered my opinion of humanity, something I didn't think possible. The grief and the guilt were strong, but gratitude was strongest; gratitude to a man who cared enough about us to send us away and turn us back on ourselves. In fact, our own problems were catching up with us and they had to be dealt with.

Eventually, a delegation of PRS loyalists showed up at our doorstep. They tried to convince Ronnie to come back, to take PRS over. They hastened to add they were okay with his long hair. New generation and all that. Now this made me nervous, to say the least. Ronnie had rescued the damsel; would he now try to rescue the castle?

Ronnie told them Mr. Hall's clear instructions to him to leave and not return. Undaunted, they insisted the circumstances justified breaking that agreement. When Ronnie continued to refuse, one of them warned that the very fate of the world could depend on his return to PRS. Ronnie seriously doubted that. He told them he was not the person that they had thought he was.

As they left, several of the delegation threw me accusatory looks. Ronnie got letters for another couple of years. Who can blame them? They were going through the suffering that Mr. Hall warned us about and spared us. They were watching from up close the end of their beloved era.

I find it ironic that Mr. Hall told us to call the police if the reincarnation of Queen Elizabeth refused to leave our apartment, but he wound up in a place in life where he never called the police on his own Queen Elizabeth, Fritz, the reincarnated Atlantean priest.

Later I was told that Toby, the stuffed bear, was with Mr. Hall on his bed when the police found him.

AN
OLYMPIAN GOODBYE

We decided to say a symbolic goodbye. Mr. Hall had recently republished *The Hymns of Orpheus* translated by Thomas Taylor. Ronnie decided to modernize the translation. He had studied ancient Greek that summer, enough to be able to use Liddell-Scott, the giant Oxford Dictionary of Ancient Greek. When in doubt he consulted the original text, which I often made him read out loud. But he chose to make his versions resemble Taylor's, which sometimes bore little resemblance to the original. A sort of tribute, if you will. This would be Ronnie's swan song for PRS and the Halls, dedicated to Mr. Hall, among others.

Ronnie explained to me that dapper lad Ficino believed he invoked the Renaissance when he performed the *Hymns of Orpheus,* each with corresponding incense, at the right astrological day and hour. Would I help Ronnie take his new versions out for a test drive? Oh, hell yes.

There, in a West Hollywood condo converted from a cheap apartment, at a window looking out on the other apartment buildings being converted into condos, but with some sky above and big trees including a cedar nearby, we faithfully followed Ficino's recipes one hymn a day. That's about ninety days of exploring the absurd, only to discover something mysterious and sublime.

Each day we burned the incense suggested by Ficino, or the best facsimile we could find, using the doctrine of signatures to choose replacements. I rang several Tibetan bells. I got the incense smoking. Not knowing if we were committed or we needed to be committed, we were going to forge through every single hymn. We meant it both as a tribute to those who gave us so much and as an invocation at a major crossroad. Do-it-yourself, old-timey religion.

Events started happening around the hymns. Occurrences occurred. For instance, in the flats of West Hollywood, during the *Hymn to Athena,* a great horned owl landed on the telephone pole right outside our window to look directly at us, staying for the entire hymn. Then it swooped toward our window as it flew away. We performed the *Hymn to Hermes* on a still day. Halfway through the hymn the winds whipped up out of nowhere, and the rattle of the blinds sounded like laughter. The *Hymn to Zeus,* one of several we performed under the deepening clear blue sky of late afternoon. What sounded like thunder. What looked like lightning. A storm without clouds. Aphrodite? While we performed the hymn, right under our window, a giggling couple kissed.

I know of no way to explain such a series of appropriate coincidences. Those weren't the only ones, of course. By the end we were awed and humbled by our astonishing experiment with an ancient ritual. We hoped we had not offended.

One more weird detail. Phanes Press published Ronnie's Orpheus mutations. Whoever designed the book cover didn't know that Ronnie was by then a long-haired guitarist. The drawing of Orpheus on the cover was a woodcut, centuries old: Luis Milan's *El Maestro,* frontispiece to *Libro de música de vihuela de mano intitulado El maestro,* from 1536. In it, Orpheus is shown strumming a guitar. He has long hair. Orpheus' guitar has constellations on it. A few months earlier I had glued glass beads all over Ronnie's cheap black electric guitar to look like stars. Behind Orpheus in the woodcut, a city is in flames. When the box of books arrived at our door, Los Angeles was in flames. From the same window where we had performed the hymns we now saw the glowing columns of smoke from the LA riots just a few neighborhoods away.

THE REST OF ART

Only two people reappeared in the next phase of our lives. William Dailey always welcomed us into his elegant bookstore on Melrose, even after our transformation into poor and nefarious-looking musicians in torn denim and flannel. He knew we couldn't afford to buy anything but he'd let us browse for hours. William Blake reprints by Trianon were our favorites. Sometimes he'd bring over a wonderfully rare occult item for us to enjoy. Later, we found out he was a skilled astrologer and a Buddhist meditator of high attainment. Other antiquarian bookstores we had once frequented were not so welcoming.

Arthur Johnson made a real effort to keep in touch. "Hey kids, call your Uncle Norm," he used to say with exasperation. Arthur warned us that our adventure in music was not going to be a cakewalk. He gave us our first and only guitar lesson. He built our first serious guitar, a gun metal blue Ibanez Telecaster I desecrated with glittery stickers. As we morphed into punk rockers Art recklessly encouraged us. Eventually, when we became better musicians, he recorded with us. Art got a big kick out of watching this butterfly leave her cocoon.

No one in our new world knew anything about our friendship with Mr. Hall. No one knew that our venture into music was a metaphysical experiment. When Mr. Hall said no to those possible futures Ronnie came up with, and then said yes to music, could he in any way have possibly known that was the only choice that would lead to my possible futures?

Arthur waited a long time for his true love, Patricia, long enough for her to raise her children. Together they spent some dreamy years living in Monaco just across the street from the Mediterranean, around the corner from a bookstore and a music shop.

Later in life, when Parkinson's cruelly deprived Art of his ability to play guitar and piano, he became a master on the violin and wrote a mysterious book about Paganini called *The Devil's Violin* and another, *Marilyn, My Marilyn,* a novel about Marilyn Monroe that was in pre-production for a feature film when Art passed away in 2018.

Art's battles with his body always led him to creative quantum leaps. He left behind a stack of manuscripts two feet high. Poetry, memoirs, occult essays he had never bothered to share. Online you can find dozens of his musical recordings in almost every genre, thanks to ITT Records. Arthur wasn't into the accolades; he was all about the creativity. In the last years of his life he finally wrote about his friendship with Mr. Hall. I wish he'd lived long enough to finish the book he was planning, to inspire others with disabilities to live their fullest possible lives. He had asked Ronnie to write the foreword.

So why haven't I told my Manly Hall story before? No one asked me until a few years ago. Art was one of the first, and he never stopped goading me, insisting I have a responsibility to tell what I'd seen and heard. I was looking forward to dropping the first draft on him for his birthday. I knew he'd have corrections and his own memories would bring back more of mine. I put some rich jabs in there, just like he taught me.

The afternoon that followed the morning I found out Norman Arthur Johnson had passed, I was outside walking my cat when I noticed a mockingbird peering at me very earnestly. Fortunately, kitty was preoccupied with eating grass. I praised the mockingbird's dapper style. The bird peered at me even more intently. We stared at each other awhile. But then with a slight huff the bird turned away.

I sardonically quipped, "Uncle Norm, is that you?" That mockingbird's head snapped around to stare at me again. Then the bird turned and started running toward me. A few feet away it flew up onto the carport roof above me and then back to the original spot for another staring contest.

That night, I happened to notice a violinist in the brightly lit window of a house across the canyon. The day I last saw Art in person, he recorded fiddle on a couple of my songs. The woman playing violin in the window never knew she was a message from a friend.

APPLIED METAPHYSICS

When one of the gracious editors from my first draft of this book insisted that as a reader she was entitled to know what happened next, the other editors backed her up. I believe all stories that go on much too long start with the phrase, "So, I'll make this brief."

When we first left PRS, we figured the plan must be for Ronnie to become a well-respected musician so he could bring attention to the esoteric tradition. Jimmy Page had Aleister Crowley; Ronnie had Mr. Hall. Having been a singer, Ronnie figured he'd pick up where he'd left off. And so began the search for a band. Ronnie was right back where he started the night we met.

I watched him suffer through a seemingly endless parade of hustlers, drunks, addicts, and wing nuts. Ronnie did not relish the idea of going on the road with foot soldiers of the patriarchy. How could we be partners and have equality if we were playing the traditional roles? I decided if those morons could learn to play guitar, this moron could, too. I wanted to audition for Ronnie's band. When I asked him to give me six months, he suggested we learn guitar together.

First, we needed a guitar. Ronnie's mom got a fancy new engagement ring, so she gave the one she hated to Ronnie to give to me. You may have already guessed where this is going. Ronnie's parents had a very difficult marriage so we figured the ring was probably cursed. At a pawn shop in Hollywood, we traded it for our first guitar, an amp, pedals, and cords.

We became a punk trio when we found a female drummer as willing to play, and as musically ignorant, as ourselves. Our first show was a fundraiser for a collective of zine writers who had befriended us. Cell 63 was an all-ages club in a storage unit in an industrial park in the San Fernando Valley, a stone's throw from where I was almost murdered in eleventh grade. This twist of fate of location was symbolic of my career with my band Lucid Nation. I realized that I had to heal the PTSD that I had been living with as long as I could remember.

MONTAGE

Our second show, we open for our friends, queercore legends Team Dresch, in an art gallery in downtown LA. Our third show we open for riot grrrl icons Bikini Kill in Montebello. Adrenaline rush makes our sets go by in a flash: punk show as out-of-body experience.

Playing to a packed house in Boston, all the kids know my lyrics and sing my songs with me. Hemp rallies, coffeehouses, riot grrrl conventions, warehouses, garages, living rooms, parks, college radio stations, and on the steps of government buildings. Playing background music for a spoken-word performance by Warhol Superstar Holly Woodlawn in a cafe of wrought iron and flowering vines, with a fountain in the patio. Fundraisers for Native American, LGBTQA, animal rights, Children of the Night, Peace and Justice Center, Amnesty International, New Panther Vanguard Movement, women's shelters, prison reform, suicide prevention, and Food Not Bombs. Letting the other bands use our gear. Giving money we make to fans who need it.

A great review from the Black Panther newspaper. A great review from Rolling Stone.

The girl who glares at the audience while she sits with her back against our kick drum is now a successful lawyer.

Posters of documentaries that we helped get made. One about the murdered singer Mia Zapata and her band, called *The Gits*. Edward James Olmos presents *Exile Nation: The Plastic People* about deportees living in sewers. *Viva Cuba Libre: Rap Is War* about the notorious underground Cuban hip hop poets

Los Aldeanos. *End of the Line: The Women of Standing Rock.*

Walking through Little Tokyo with my band at three o'clock in the morning, the witching hour, on a Monday night, headed to the one noodle shop we know will be open, after having just laid down a vocal that made their jaws drop. The studio dense and hot. The street cold and empty. Under the glow of a yellow sign, a few blocks away, the restaurant is almost as lit up as I am.

Driving with windows down on First Street at four o'clock Sunday morning after sixteen hours of recording. The dull orange streetlights glow on a hot summer night. Steam rises from grates. Across from the severe bureaucratic architecture of the Criminal Justice Center, that notable erection Los Angeles City Hall looms like a herm from Ancient Greece. On the left LAPD Headquarters is a bunker of sharp modern angles with walls of mirrored windows that look like they were made by the same company that makes policemen's sunglasses. Not another car in sight. The cats of downtown LA that no one ever sees recline in the street with complete confidence that at this hour it belongs to them. They leave enough space so that I can slowly maneuver through without them having to move. They watch with casual curiosity. A dozen feral cats enjoying the warm asphalt in the heart of Los Angeles just before dawn.

END MONTAGE

One night we played to an empty club in Little Tokyo, just down the street from the *kendo* where, after spending twenty years without revealing his attainment, Zen master Nyogen Senzaki offered the sudden enlightenment of *satori* to LA. The proprietor liked our music so he asked us to keep playing after our set. We didn't have any more songs. "Make something up," he said. "We ain't got no place to go."

The old neon Atomic Cafe sign leaned against the wall in the back patio of the club now named Impala. In chained-up parking lots the streetlights glowed on emptiness. Vicious dogs dozed. Old dank brick warehouses slept nearby, leaving you to wonder how they could have survived the earthquakes. Cheerfully decorated Japanese businesses were now dimmed behind security bars. You could easily imagine a body found in one of the alienated and anonymous office buildings, devoid of architectural style.

Ronnie looked at me and shrugged. He conjured rhythm and melody on bass, and the drummer joined in. I remembered a story Mr. Hall told me. About the Bodhisattva's leap of faith. To simply step into the unknown and realize that you don't fall. I took up the challenge. First a riff, then a lyric, then a song unfolded that sounded like a far better band than us had written it. You would have sworn we had rehearsed that song for a year. When we finished, the proprietor smiled and said: "That's your best song. What's it called?" We didn't know, and we could never play it again. As soon as it appeared it was gone. But we've recorded many others. Our in-the-moment inventions are always better than the songs we compose. We improvised our most popular record, the only one to hit number one on college radio.

EPILOGUE

I. CONTEXT

Of the tragedies that occurred to the Halls at the end, one of the most haunting, is that Mr. Hall wanted to move PRS, due to a fear that an earthquake or some other disaster would destroy all the treasures he had collected. I believe Fritz probably instilled that fear in him, but that's just a guess. The reason that we had first gone to PRS was Ronnie's own foreboding of geological disaster. Mr. Hall had cured that, only to succumb to it himself. Nobody was there to help him relax away from it. But I know he wouldn't want us to dwell on the morbid details, nor should anyone. That wasn't the work he left behind. His work was distilling the beauty and wisdom he found in rare manuscripts and books into a philosophy of life that was gentle, healthy, and rewarding. His eloquence made his books and lectures a joyful aesthetic experience, as anyone can find out for themselves on YouTube.

Online message boards have some wild ideas about him. Mr. Hall was an evil Illuminati overlord, for example. He was a Luciferian working to undermine Christian society. A bisexual hermaphrodite, he hustled old ladies for money. Arthur reported that the old man had a keen eye for shapely female derrieres. Our friend Loreen, when she told me about PRS and started this mess, claimed young Mr. Hall spent his weekends having trysts with female admirers. Ronnie and

I never saw anything like any of that, but of course we weren't there then. Maybe the old man was on his best behavior with us, though I don't know why he should have been. Perhaps he had mellowed with age.

There's also the paradox of the Manly Hall I knew who strongly disapproved of hippies when he saw them on TV, versus the Manly Hall of the 1960s who helped Source Restaurant guru Father Yod name his bevy of hippie brides. Including our dear friend Isis Aquarian, to whom I owe thanks for encouraging me to write this book.

I've noticed most modern occult authors don't seem to know the work of Catherine Albanese. Her book *A Republic of Mind and Spirit*, published by Yale in 2007, reminds me of *The Secret Teachings of All Ages*; they both survey the same Hermetic timeline. Reading the two books together would be a lot of fun. But Professor Albanese is missing from most recent occult bibliographies. Maybe that's prejudice against academics, not women? Who can blame occultists for feeling wary of academics after so many years of neglect and ridicule?

As a former riot grrrl I asked my academic friends if they knew of any studies about feminism in American Metaphysical Religion or the occult in general. No one had heard of any. The only essay I could find was "There's not much room for women in esotericism, right?" by Allison P. Courdet in *Hermes Explains: Thirty Questions About Western Esotericism,* published by Amsterdam University Press in 2019. At long last Palgrave Macmillan in 2021 released *Essays on Women in Western Esotericism: Beyond Seeresses and Sea Priestesses,* edited by esoteric scholar Amy Hale.

I wonder, was Manly Hall a feminist? He married one. At the end of his life independent women ran everything at PRS except shipping. You could argue that PRS was feminist by attrition. Unbeknownst to us, two of the men who ran it had recently died, and another left for a more lucrative career. Still, as many female as male teachers taught classes at PRS, at least when I was there. Mr. Hall didn't treat Ronnie and me differently. But perhaps there's better evidence of his feminism than that. A flyer from the early 1950s announces: "Manly Palmer Hall presents Marie Bauer Hall in a class of twelve interrelated lessons: Birth of a New Age & The Pattern of The Living Way." Tuition fee one dollar per class. Each class title is accompanied by a quote from the usual suspects: Bacon, Shakespeare, Wither, *The Sonnets of G.S.0.*, and, of course, the Holy Bible.

The series took place Monday evenings at the Friday Morning Club, a women's club founded by Caroline Severance. When female Californians got the right to vote in 1911, they celebrated Caroline as the spiritual leader of their movement. The Friday Morning Club also hosted non-feminist lectures, of course; their goal was cultural enrichment. But when Manly Hall produced a lecture series for his feminist wife at a women's club founded by a suffragist, that's about as progressive as a guy could get between the first and second waves of feminism.

PRS was a place where a spontaneous conversation could change the direction of a life. It reminded me of bees communicating where to find flowers. Of course, we were seeing only the best in everyone, but for a long time the best was all there was to see. We seemed to arrive when Mr. Hall and PRS had ripened to tranquility, with no hint yet of the moribund future. Peaceful days. Like late autumn, when the sun glitters golden over all creation, the stones still keep a trace of warmth from summer, and the fragrances of the harvest haven't yet faded in the cold of winter. During this quiet moment when Mr. Hall's powerful friends had mostly gone to their just rewards, he and PRS were at their most accessible and humble. Mr. Hall had socialized with governors, mayors, famous actors, retired military officers, Beverly Hills lawyers, and oil heiresses. For a time the PRS Board of Trustees even boasted an astronaut who walked on the moon, Edgar Mitchell. At any other time I doubt the likes of us would have made it past that door with the sign that said: "Private."

II. UNANSWERABLE QUESTIONS

Was there something mystical or magical about MPH? Well, there was that weird knack of lecturing right at strangers about their problems. Strangers he couldn't see very well. He had an ability to bounce like a sprite off serendipity. I heard stories from old-timers who claimed in his early days he showed off *siddhis,* or powers allegedly associated with yogis, holy men, and occultists. Recently, Joseph Lucido, a well-known guitarist around Monterey, California, told me about experiences his own teacher Madora Krauzlis had when she was Mr. Hall's student, way back before Mr. Hall married his first wife. Madora said Mr. Hall's advice not to practice ceremonial magic came from his own experience. She also told Joe of an occasion when Mr. Hall "psychically zapped" a guy who was stalking her.

I experienced a more subtle magic. Without Manly and Marie Hall's friendships I wonder if I would have remained silent all my life, like that ominous majority, steeped in the resentments of the unexamined life.

Marie was much more than mad. Both kinds. Academics haven't gotten around to Manly Hall, let alone Marie, but maybe someday Marie will receive the scholarship that may find in her divine madness characteristics typical of a long line of female Christian mystics. If you'd like to know more about Marie's work, hunt down a book called *God As Mother* by Victoria Jennings, the metaphysician who was allowed to make copies of Marie's cosmic diagrams. After Mr. Hall's death, Jennings pursued an understanding of Marie's philosophy with great devotion for six years, taping all their conversations. Marie's faculties had begun to fade, but Victoria managed to preserve her teachings. Near the end of her life Marie moved in with her family. She gave up saving the world. She watched the flickering images of old sitcoms on television instead. She lived to be one hundred years old.

◈

I wonder if Fritz entered his friendship with the Halls with the best of intentions, because the road to hell is paved with those. Opinions tend to fall to one side or the other. Fritz meant well. He helped Mr. Hall lose weight and exercise. He was a can-do guy who knew how to start companies, he understood the potential of computer networks. He thought he was the reincarnation of an Atlantean priest. And so it was his fate to give care to Mr. Hall, help Marie use computers to connect with the world, assist them in crossing over, and protect their legacies as the legal representative of both their nonprofits and the millions of dollars' worth of assets attached.

Many people think Fritz was a criminal who committed senior abuse, fraud, grand larceny, and murder. I find intriguing the possibility that Fritz was all those things. Perhaps, trying his best, he unleashed a series of tragedies. If he didn't commit crimes as part of a deliberate plot, he is an example of the havoc that happens when love-and-light New Agers succumb to their shadows.

In the twenty-first century you can find the mysteries on your favorite search engine. Not so in the twentieth. Manly Palmer Hall gave the wisdom, once for the few, to the many. Best of all, the numerous video and audio recordings of his lectures can be enjoyed for free online where they have millions of views. The comments are for the most part grateful.

Some have suggested that perhaps Mr. Hall wasn't that wise after all, since he fell into the trap of an obvious grifter. They think that he didn't realize what was happening or, if he did, only when it was too late.

In a meeting with the PRS Trustees just before his death in 1990, Mr. Hall joked that everyone should accommodate Fritz, but he referred to him as the High Lord Executioner. I suspect he was referencing the Lord High Executioner in the Gilbert and Sullivan musical *The Mikado*. Mr. Hall also got that wrong in 1950, in the winter issue of his journal *Horizon,* where he wrote: "It may be more than a merry jest of the High Lord Executioner in *The Mikado* that when natural laws are violated the punishment fits the crime." The song "Behold the Lord High Executioner" includes this verse sung by the character:

> *"Taken from the county jail*
> *By a set of curious chances;*
> *Liberated then on bail*
> *On my own recognizances."*

That sure was an interesting nickname for Mr. Hall to give Fritz.

Whatever they say about Mr. Hall's past, or the future that I never saw, the man I knew was one of the most decent human beings I have ever met. The following paragraph, which he wrote for the *PRS Journal* winter 1986 edition, explains his wisdom better than I ever could.

Because of my reticence in discussing my own beliefs, I am frequently asked what religion I follow—what spiritual revelation has inspired my activities. The simple fact is that I sincerely believe that I am serving with the best of my ability the dictates of my own conscience. My daily work is my discipline, and I am making no effort to advance my own spiritual destiny. There seems to be no need to limit or restrict the normal actions of other human beings. My teacher has been the very public I am seeking to serve. Thousands of troubled persons have sought my advice or assistance and in each case I have gained new and deeper insight into the workings of human thoughts and emotions. I know opinionated individuals who insisted on going their own way and who came in the end to wish they had followed the advice they had formerly rejected. I have lectured in hospitals, prisons, Christian churches, and Jewish synagogues. I have baptized and christened the new born; performed inter-religious marriages which various churches refused to solemnize. I have been called to the bedside of the sick, comforted the dying, and performed funerals and memorial services. These are the sources by which an understanding of life is enriched and there is very little justification for antagonism, intolerance, or bigotry.

And so I built this obelisk. And now dear reader, in honor of your patience, I reward you with something sweet. Feel free to substitute healthier ingredients.

"MAD MARIE'S" ZUCCHINI PANCAKE RECIPE

Marie used the recipe straight from the Bisquick box: "Classic Pancakes. Makes 14." But there's more.

First, add one-half teaspoon of cinnamon to two cups of Bisquick. Whisk it. In a mesh colander, with your hand, squeeze the excess water out of one cup of shredded zucchini. Place shredded zucchini on several layers of paper towels for further drying. Use the paper towels to squeeze out as much of the moisture as you can. Mix the shredded zucchini with the Bisquick mixture until all the zucchini is coated. Beat together one cup milk and two eggs, along with one teaspoon of vanilla extract. Now pour the liquid ingredients into the dry. Don't over mix!

Pour the batter onto a hot, greased griddle, just under one-quarter cup at a time. Once the edges are dry, flip them and cook until they're golden.

Serve with butter and hot maple syrup.

Discover the taste of one of Mr. Hall's favorite treats. Bon appétit!

ABOUT THE AUTHOR

After her seven years of friendship with Manly P. Hall, in 1994 Tamra started the band Lucid Nation, making a splash in the punk rock scene. Lucid Nation has played riot grrrl conventions, Black Panther fundraisers, Food Not Bombs shows, and art galleries alongside icons like Bikini Kill and Holly Woodlawn. Tamra's zine writing was published in several compilations, including *A Girl's Guide to Taking Over the World: Writings from the Girl Zine Revolution, Zine Scene,* and *Riot Grrrl: Revolution Girl Style Now!*

In 2002 Tamra became art editor of Newtopia Magazine, then the principal interviewer for the original Reality Sandwich. Her interview subjects have included presidential candidates Marianne Williamson and Gov. Buddy Roemer, Oscar-nominated director of Food Inc. Robbie Kenner, activist and poet John Trudell, and Kelly Heresy of Occupy Wall Street. Tamra's zine writing was published in several compilations, including *A Girl's Guide to Taking Over the World: Writings from the Girl Zine Revolution, Zine Scene,* and *Riot Grrrl: Revolution Girl Style Now!*

Tamra has produced documentary films that include *Exile Nation: The Plastic People,* executive produced and narrated by Edward James Olmos, *End of the Line: The Women of Standing Rock,* and *Viva Cuba Libre: Rap Is War,* an award-winning documentary about Cuban hip hop legends Los Aldeanos.